INTERMEDIATE 2 & HIGHER
Physical Education

grade **booster**

Malcolm Thorburn

D0242394

Text © 2006 Malcolm Thorburn
Design and layout © 2006 Leckie & Leckie
Cover image © Up the Resolution (uptheres) / Alamy

02/06072007

ISBN 978-1-84372-383-7

Published by
Leckie & Leckie Ltd, 3rd floor, 4 Queen Street, Edinburgh, EH2 1JE
Tel: 0131 220 6831 Fax: 0131 225 9987
enquiries@leckieandleckie.co.uk   www.leckieandleckie.co.uk

Special thanks to
Caleb Rutherford (cover design), BRW (creative packaging),
Pumpkin House (design and page make-up)
Tom Hardie (content review), Roda Morrison (copy-edit & proofread).

A CIP Catalogue record for this book is available from the British Library.

Leckie & Leckie Ltd is a division of Huveaux plc.

Acknowledgements
Leckie & Leckie is grateful to the copyright holders, as credited, for permission to use their material: The Scottish Qualifications Authority for permission to reproduce past examination questions. (Answers do not emanate from the SQA.)

Every effort has been made to trace the copyright holders and to obtain their permission for the use of copyright material. Leckie & Leckie will gladly receive information enabling them to rectify any error or omission in subsequent editions.

CONTENTS

CONTENTS continued

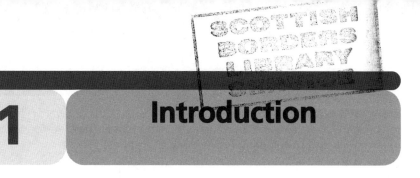

1 Introduction

Why do I need this book?

Unit / Course outline and assessment

What this book covers

WHY DO I NEED THIS BOOK?

Intermediate 2 and Higher Level Physical Education Grade Booster has four aims. These are to help you understand

- the specific skills you require for the analysis and development of performance
- the relevant concepts involved in Physical Education at Intermediate 2 and Higher level
- the assessment process and national standards of assessment
- how to achieve the highest pass grade possible.

Analysis matters in Physical Education

Analysis is a major part of sport in the media. There is great interest in performance and in whether teams and individual sportspersons perform to their potential. *Intermediate 2 and Higher Level Physical Education* focuses on your performance and on analysing and developing your performance.

 Remember: analysis in Higher Still Physical Education is on **your** own performance.

UNIT / COURSE OUTLINE AND ASSESSMENT

Higher Still qualifications are made up of **Units** and **Course awards**. Two Units make up a Course award at Intermediate 2 and Higher level: Performance Unit and Analysis and Development of Performance Unit.

Performance Unit

You are assessed by your teacher in the different activities. If you achieve the Performance Unit, you can use it as part of your Course award in Physical Education.

Analysis and Development of Performance Unit

The four areas of Analysis and Development of Performance are:

Area 1   Performance Appreciation

Area 2   Preparation of the Body

Area 3   Skills and Techniques

Area 4   Structures, Strategies and Composition

Key points to remember

✔ Your Analysis and Development of Performance will include the study of at least three of these areas.

✔ Each of these areas of Analysis and Development of Performance is made up of a number of **Key Concepts**.

✔ To achieve a Unit in Analysis and Development of Performance you will be assessed in your Centre (School / College) by your teacher.

✔ The Course Assessment is by a written examination. In this examination you need to complete three answers, each from a different area of Analysis and Development of Performance.

✔ The examination at Intermediate 2 level lasts two hours.

✔ At Higher level the examination lasts two and a half hours.

Assessment

- To achieve a Unit you have to complete successfully the Unit Assessments.
- To achieve the Course award, i.e. Physical Education at Intermediate 2 or Higher level, you have to complete successfully the Unit Assessments and the Course award Assessments at the chosen level of presentation.

Course award aggregation

When you complete all the Course Assessments a final mark will be calculated. This final mark is based on the following weighting:

Performance counts as 40% of your final mark at Higher level, 50% at Intermediate 2 level.

Analysis and Development of Performance counts as 60% of your final mark at Higher level, 50% at Intermediate 2 level.

You can achieve a Course award with an 'A', 'B' or 'C' pass depending on your final mark.

WHAT THIS BOOK COVERS

Intermediate 2 and Higher Level Physical Education Grade Booster is divided into ten chapters.

This Introductory chapter outlines the course and assessment, and gives you information about how the book is organised.

Chapter 2 contains introductory information on beginning your Analysis and Development of Performance.

Chapters 3–6 study each of the four learning outcomes involved in the Analysis and Development of Performance (investigating, analysing, developing and reviewing / evaluating performance).

Chapter 7 provides you with greater detail about how to improve your analysis work overall.

Chapter 8 helps you with assessment preparation advice.

Chapter 9 helps you to prepare for your Analysis and Development of Performance examination.

Chapter 10 provides assessment examples from each of the four different areas of Analysis and Development of Performance.

A Key Words Checklist is provided at the end of the book for reference.

An integrated approach

- In chapters 3 to 6 four examples of performance-related study are provided.
- Each example links activities to different areas of Analysis and Development of Performance.
- Follow these examples, defined by the 'jigsaw' icon, as you complete the process of investigating, analysing, developing and reviewing / evaluating performance.
- This reflects the learning and assessment approach which you will complete when answering your examination questions.

Other icons used in this book

Top Tip

Worked example

Recap

Setting goals

2 Beginning Your Analysis and Development of Performance

The design model for Analysis and Development of Performance

An integrated approach

Introductory considerations in the Analysis and Development of Performance

The Cycle of Analysis

THE DESIGN MODEL FOR ANALYSIS AND DEVELOPMENT OF PERFORMANCE

The diagram below shows how the four areas of Analysis and Development of Performance relate to each other. Performance Appreciation takes a general overview of Performance and all that it includes. The other three areas look at specific areas of performance.

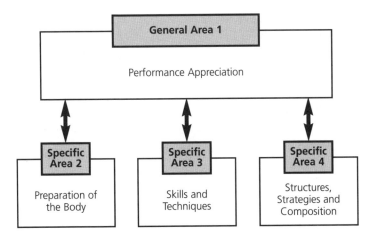

General Area 1

Performance Appreciation

Specific Area 2 — Preparation of the Body

Specific Area 3 — Skills and Techniques

Specific Area 4 — Structures, Strategies and Composition

Note how the two-way arrows in the diagram link Performance Appreciation to the three other areas. Each area includes a number of Key Concepts. When you are studying Key Concepts within Performance Appreciation, consider how they relate to specific Key Concepts in the other three areas. Likewise, when studying Area 2, 3 or 4, relate your work in that area to Key Concepts in Area 1.

Understanding this link between areas is essential at the outset of your Analysis and Development of Performance work. Do not, however, link together Key Concepts from across the three specific areas.

> The key point to remember is that your Analysis and Development of Performance work will involve you in linking your understanding from the general to the specific and from the specific to the general.

Your teacher will explain to you, which performance activities relate to the different areas of Analysis and Development of Performance. Understanding this relationship is very important. If you are unsure, ask!

AN INTEGRATED APPROACH

Consider this example. In working practically at basketball, your Analysis and Development of Performance could cover some aspects of Performance Appreciation in general and Preparation of the Body in specific detail.

In Performance Appreciation your Analysis of Performance could cover the Key Concepts of 'the overall nature and demands of quality performance' and the 'mental factors influencing performance'. So, your Analysis and Development of Performance could include:

- nature of basketball, e.g. team, set rules, expected codes of conduct (nature / demands)
- performance demands, e.g. different roles, working to your potential (nature / demands)
- managing your emotions during demanding performance (mental factors)
- intrinsic motivation to perform well (mental factors)

When studying Preparation of the Body in basketball, your Analysis and Development of Performance will cover all of the Key Concepts in this area. As an example of integration, the two Key Concepts of 'physical, skill-related and mental aspects of fitness' and 'principles and methods of training' could link to basketball by including:

- specific physical fitness demands of different roles in basketball (physical fitness)
- reacting quickly to the movements of the opposing team when defending (skill-related fitness)
- applying principles of specificity and progressive overload (principles / methods)
- combining methods of physical and skill-related fitness (principles / methods)

(Other Key Concepts in Preparation of the Body would be covered in a similar way.)

INTRODUCTORY CONSIDERATIONS IN THE ANALYSIS AND DEVELOPMENT OF PERFORMANCE

Your Analysis and Development of Performance work should relate to your Performance improvement work. As you work practically, you will also be learning about relevant Key Concepts in Analysis and Development of Performance.

To help you do this:

- start by identifying your current level of ability (skills / fitness) and your experience of the activity
- keep your practical work closely related to the demands of 'whole' performance
- set the purpose for your practice / game / performance work
- allow time for meaningful performance improvement and understanding of relevant Key Concepts to occur
- build some progression into your practice / game / performance work
- realise that more and more of the same practice is usually not as beneficial as a set of better organised, carefully constructed progressive practices
- have an ongoing review of the practical set-up or 'environment' you are working in – is it useful for what you are intending?

The example below shows the link between Performance in volleyball and Analysis of Performance in Skills and Techniques: it shows how performing in volleyball links with studying the different Key Concepts in Skills and Techniques.

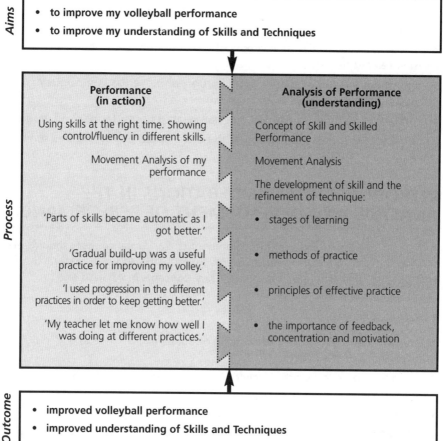

Aims

- to improve my volleyball performance
- to improve my understanding of Skills and Techniques

Process

Performance (in action)	Analysis of Performance (understanding)
Using skills at the right time. Showing control/fluency in different skills.	Concept of Skill and Skilled Performance
Movement Analysis of my performance	Movement Analysis
	The development of skill and the refinement of technique:
'Parts of skills became automatic as I got better.'	• stages of learning
'Gradual build-up was a useful practice for improving my volley.'	• methods of practice
'I used progression in the different practices in order to keep getting better.'	• principles of effective practice
'My teacher let me know how well I was doing at different practices.'	• the importance of feedback, concentration and motivation

Outcome

- improved volleyball performance
- improved understanding of Skills and Techniques

THE CYCLE OF ANALYSIS

The Cycle of Analysis is one popular approach that is useful for analysing and developing your performance as part of your performance improvement programme. Using the Cycle of Analysis, you collect information about your performance in an organised way. In this way you identify and assess specific aspects of your performance.

Study the four stages of the Cycle of Analysis in diagram 1. These four stages can be applied effectively to your own activities. Diagram 2 shows the complete cycle of analysis.

By using the Cycle of Analysis, you can continue to improve your performance and so avoid reaching a learning plateau – a stage of no apparent progress.

 You should design training programmes that allow your performance to show consistent progress. This is better than inconsistent improvement caused by learning plateaux. Diagram 3 outlines how applying the Cycle of Analysis can lead to ongoing improvement in performance.

The diagram below shows the four stages of the Cycle of Analysis.

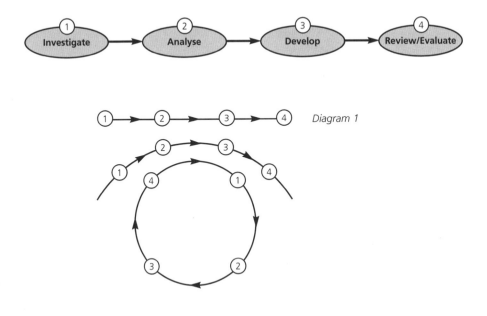

Diagram 1

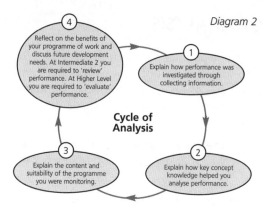

Diagram 2

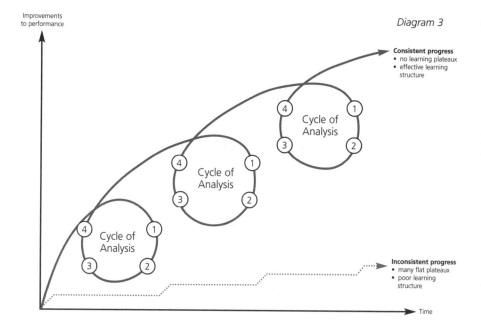

Diagram 3

3 Investigating Performance

Methods of collecting information

Observation schedules

Video of performances

Reflections about your performance

Knowledge of results

Using a dictaphone

Error detection / correction

Game analysis

Improving your Investigation of Performance (Intermediate 2 level)

Improving your Investigation of Performance (Higher level)

Marked examples of Investigation of Performance (Higher level)

METHODS OF COLLECTING INFORMATION

Collecting valid information is the vital first step when analysing performance. The information you collect must:

be **specific** to your performance and to your performance level

relate to your Analysis and Development of Performance areas.

For example, if you are a very competent footballer, information about your fitness for your performance will come from a competitive situation. This will ensure that the information is **accurate**. If your cardiorespiratory fitness is being measured, the information is collected by measuring your respiratory rates during competitive play. This information about your performance can then be used to plan your improvement programme.

To design a skills-based training programme you would collect a **different** form of information. For example, if you were looking at your effectiveness in passing then it would be useful to collect information about the timing, accuracy, disguise and weight of your different passes. If you were evaluating your team's performance from a strategy perspective, you would collect another different form of information.

> You can collect information by using: observation schedules, videos of performances, reflections on your performance, knowledge of results, using a dictaphone, error detection / correction and game analysis.

OBSERVATION SCHEDULES

Observation schedules record information about your performance. You are observed performing and a record of your performance is made. Developing the criteria against which your performance is going to be judged is the most important initial consideration. The evidence that you gain from performance has to be **valid, reliable** and **straightforward to interpret**.

Study the two examples of observation schedules on pages 18 and 19. The first example, on page 18, looks at the effectiveness of someone playing an overhead clear shot in badminton. Repeated observation of the performer allows the observer to make a record of the performer's strengths and weaknesses, relative to the criteria. The criteria are quite specific and this allows for a detailed stroke analysis. A second assessment at a later date against the same criteria can then be recorded to show the degree of progress that has occurred. This format is particularly useful for measuring and analysing a **single technique**.

With this format, you need to ensure that the performance setting is suited to your level of ability. In this example, this would usually mean that you were playing against or practising with an opponent of similar ability. This helps add to the accuracy of the results. If this is difficult to arrange, you can often use a teacher or classmate. She could then feed the shuttlecock to exactly where it is needed and at the speed and direction required for you to collect valid information.

The second example on page 19 shows information collected the performance of a spike in a game of volleyball. This format for collecting information is useful for game analysis because it shows the results of each spike played. Information from this schedule enables analysis of a player's strengths and weaknesses from different sets, for different angles of spike and against different degrees of opposition. In this example you start from the top of the schedule and record relevant details. First you enter whether or not the point was won from the spike (i.e. was it effective or ineffective?). Then further definition is added: you record information about the angle of the spike, the degree of opposition and the type of set provided. As a result of this observation, you can gain an accurate portrayal of a player's effectiveness in spiking.

Observation schedule

Scotstown Academy
Intermediate 2 and Higher Level Physical Education – Observation Schedule
Technique Analysis to identify Strengths/Weaknesses

Date: 00/00/00 Venue: <u>Sports hall</u> Assessor: <u>Steven Turnbull S6</u> Role: <u>Classmate, Badminton doubles partner</u>
Performance Context: This checklist was completed during competitive practice with classmate of similar ability
called Zanab Patel. During specified drills my overhead clear was assessed in a 1 hour session.

SKILL: _DEFENSIVE SHOT_   TECHNIQUE: _Overhead Clear_

Essential Features	Model Performer	Self Date 1	Self Date 2	Additional comments
PREPARATION				
1 Move to get sideways on	✓	?	✓	
2 Complete backswing of racket	✓	✓	✓	
3 Non-hitting hand points at shuttle	✓	?	✓	
4 Weight over back foot	✓	✗	?	
5 Watch shuttle closely	✓	✓	✓	
ACTION				
1 Wide range of shoulder movement	✓	✓	✓	
2 Speed of racket head – power in shot	✓	✓	✓	
3 Transfer of weight onto front foot	✓	✗	?	
4 Arm straightened to hit shuttle	✓	?	?	
5 Elbow leading hitting action	✓	?	?	
RECOVERY				
1 Follow through in the direction of shuttle	✓	✓	✓	
2 Move forward to mid-court	✓	✗	?	
3 Weight evenly balanced on balls of feet	✓	?	✓	
4 Racket in central ready position	✓	?	✓	
5 Anticipating next shot	✓	✗	?	

Criteria to be used for assessing performance
✓ = highly effective – fluent, controlled, etc.
? = limited effectiveness – needs improvement
✗ = ineffective – needs considerable improvement

Observation schedule

Scotstown Academy
Intermediate 2 and Higher Level Physical Education – Observation Schedule
Technique Analysis to identify Strengths/Weaknesses

Date: 00/00/00 Venue: <u>School Sports hall</u> Assessor: <u>Ms M McDonald</u> Role: <u>Teacher</u>
Performance Context: This checklist was completed during an inter-school tournament. The games were 4 v 4 games which allowed many spikes to be attempted.

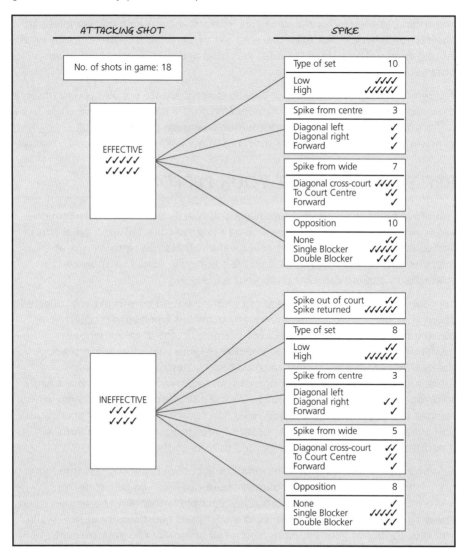

VIDEO OF PERFORMANCES

A video recording of a performance is very useful for compiling evidence because it allows you to view a performance repeatedly, and often in slow motion. Slow motion replay is a considerable advantage when the speed of a performance makes recording observations at normal speeds difficult: slowing down the fast and complex action of the tennis serve, for example, allows you to make a detailed technique analysis.

You could use a video recording of your performance to help you complete an observation schedule. For example, your performance as a centre in rugby when kicking from defence could be video recorded and then analysed using an observation schedule.

A video recording of your own or another's performance enables you to observe movements more accurately. Remember to consider the position and angle from which you are collecting video information to ensure that it is useful. This allows you to identify clearly the strengths and weaknesses of the performance.

REFLECTIONS ABOUT YOUR PERFORMANCE

Subjective feelings about performance are also very important. Reflecting on your own performance can often support evidence collected from other sources. You could do this if you felt that your level of fitness was restricting your improvement in performance or if you felt that your ability to apply certain strategies in a game contributed to your success.

Your subjective thoughts and feelings can also be used as information collected about your performance. There are many occasions when strictly objective-based information is not required. For example, in the development of a modern dance motif or a gymnastic sequence, your subjective feelings about the qualities of your performance could best be described by personal reflection. This is because the design of your improvement programme is likely to be open-ended (i.e. you are not following a set formula). Instead, you are using your **imagination** and **critical reflection** to work out ways to enhance your performance. You should keep a record of your thoughts and reflections, e.g. in a performance diary, in order to be able to refer to them.

One of the best ways to collect information about your reflections is through a **questionnaire**. A well- designed questionnaire can help you reflect on key performance issues and help you to assess your performance. For example, when assessing your mental fitness you could ask yourself questions about how well you kept control of your emotions, your level of arousal and your concentration.

KNOWLEDGE OF RESULTS

Knowledge of results is also very useful as a measurement of performance. You can use information about results in all four areas of Analysis and Development of Performance.

For example, knowledge of results about success rates in short corners in hockey is useful when discussing both Skills and Techniques, and Structures, Strategies and Composition. The information collected could relate to success rates at completing the different passing and hitting techniques. It could also relate to information about the strengths and weaknesses of using different players in different positions at short corners. In these examples, using knowledge of previous performances is an important part of collecting knowledge of results information.

Knowledge of results can also be useful for collecting information about Preparation of the Body (e.g. your level of cardiorespiratory endurance). In most games a high level of cardiorespiratory endurance is required to cope with the high work rate of the body over long periods of time. Monitoring your heart rate provides information about your level of cardiorespiratory fitness.

These two tennis players can record data about their heart rates during a game, using heart rate monitors. The data can then be analysed on computer (see diagrams below).

Data from player 1's Heart Rate Monitor showing effective training

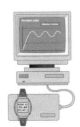

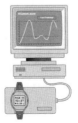

Data from player 2's Heart Rate Monitor showing poor training

If your work rate drops during the later stages of a game, your heart rate also drops. Knowing these figures can help you plan a training programme related to the specific cardiorespiratory demands of the performance. Collected evidence could then be matched to your training zone as shown in the diagram on page 21. Improvements in your level of cardiorespiratory fitness could be measured against previous performances in games.

USING A DICTAPHONE

Using a dictaphone is another effective method of collecting information about your performance. This method is useful as it allows you to immediately record your thoughts with minimal interruption. It can sometimes interrupt the flow of your performance if you pause for too long a time. Hence, a dictaphone is helpful as it allows you to capture some significant specific comments about your performance in a short unfussy way. It is also useful as it allows you to listen to the replays of the tape when it suits you.

ERROR DETECTION / CORRECTION

After an initial observation of your performance it is useful for you (on your own or with your teacher) to analyse your performance over a period of time. This will help you evaluate your performance and establish whether your performance is becoming more accurate and consistent. Analysing performance over a period of time helps identify whether there are specific errors within your performance which require to be corrected.

Diagram 1 highlights the performance qualities and criteria required for effective court movement in badminton. The teacher comments complied for the second assessment have detected that the overall performance weakness (error) is the student's difficulty with their posture and balance. The student still requires getting a little lower and flexed. From this error detection analysis a number of correction remedies are possible. This could involve: repeating again the same analysis with further teacher commentary at a later date; defining further qualitative performance criteria for more detailed error detection analysis of posture and balance or alternatively completing a quantitative measurement of performance. This might be useful as it would enable a combination of qualitative and quantitative data to be collected.

Diagram 1

Name: Denise Scott		Date: 00/00/00	
Qualities needed	Court movement criteria	Teacher comment 1st assessment	Teacher comment 2nd assessment
Posture and balance	Body is well centred in preparation for moving	Sometimes your movements begin when you have not established a clear base position	Getting better — still some need to get a little lower and flexed
	Moves early to play shuttle in all directions	Taking smaller initial steps would help balance when moving	Beginning to move away from base in a better posture, especially backwards
	Neat tidy footwork	Footwork is better when a few steps are linked together	Again better when steps are linked
	Body is relaxed, flexed and ready to move	Slightly tense look at times	Looking more relaxed when you have time
Starting and stopping	Can accelerate quickly from a standing start going forwards	Movement is quite fast — greater control is needed	Good, fast — getting more control
	Can accelerate quickly from a standing start going backwards	Slightly arched back leading to poor starting position	Much better. You're starting to move more effectively through better posture and balance
	Can accelerate quickly from a standing start going sideways	Slightly better moving sideways	Again good moving in in this direction
	Can remain stable when preparing to play shots	Slightly more open flexed base of support required	Slightly more stable when getting 'set up'
Travelling	Movement in all directions is fluent	Once movement has begun some fluency is evident	Movement again is good when travelling
	Has 'soft feet' when moving	Large steps sometimes lead to 'loud' long steps	Better balance when travelling — good
Lunge and recovery	Can reach and stretch in balance to play shots	Long reach is helping you to recover shots	Reach as ever is good
	Can transfer weight backwards to recover	Slightly slow at beginning your transfer of weight to get back to centre of court	Recovery time is getting better especially when returning from the back of the court

Diagram 2

Details of the agility runs and times completed on court

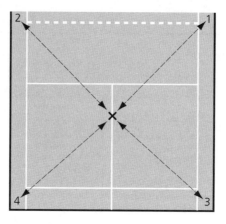

Diagram 3

		1st attempt	2nd attempt	3rd attempt	1st attempt average	2nd attempt average
1	Base (x) to front forehand corner at start of training	3.7s	3.8s	3.9s	3.8s	
1	Base to front forehand corner at end of training	3.5s	3.5s	3.8s		3.6s
2	Base to front backhand corner at start of training	3.8s	3.6s	4.1s	3.9s	
2	Base to front backhand corner at end of training	3.6s	3.6s	3.9s		3.7s
3	Base to back forehand corner at start of training	4.0s	3.9s	4.3s	4.1s	
3	Base to back forehand corner at end of training	3.8s	3.7s	3.9s		3.8s
4	Base to back backhand corner at start of training	4.2s	4.3s	4.1s	4.2s	
4	Base to back backhand corner at end of training	3.8s	3.8s	3.8s		3.8s

Diagrams 2 and 3 are examples of how this could be completed for effective court movement in badminton. Completing these agility-based movement practices would indicate whether the effect that posture and balance (along with other performance qualities) was having on your court speed was improving or not.

GAME ANALYSIS

Game analysis is a useful way of using statistical information to analyse performance. In the example on page 26 a range of general and specific information is available which can 'paint a picture' of how previous tennis matches between two players have been decided.

With this type of information you should be able to analyse your own performance in ways which relate to all the different areas of Analysis and Development of Performance.

- Within Performance Appreciation, information about your second serve effectiveness and number of double faults might highlight whether any particular mental factors were influencing your performance. A high return rate would indicate that you are able to manage your emotions well and a low return rate might indicate some anxiety in your performance.

- Within Preparation of the Body, first services 'in' and first service points won is an indicator of different aspects of fitness: physical fitness (power); skill-related fitness (timing) and mental aspects of fitness (rehearsal). Sustained first service effectiveness indicates that your overall fitness is high and low service speeds indicate otherwise.

- Within Skills and Techniques, analysis of the different stroke techniques (volleys, drives, smash) indicates the relative strengths and weaknesses of your overall tennis performance.

- Within Structures, Strategies and Composition, an analysis of your tactics through considering the percentage of shots which were won at the net or from the baseline is useful in highlighting whether you were playing the type of game you considered when preparing for the game.

Tennis: Game analysis

Player A	Performanc criterion		Player B	
1.75m	Height		1.83m	
	Weight			
Right-handed	Plays		Left-handed	
	Previous Matches			
Year	**Tournament**	**Surface**	**Stage**	**Winner**	**Score**

Year	Tournament	Surface	Stage	Winner	Score
2003	Local League	Hard	QF	Player A	4-6, 6-3, 6-3
2004	Club Championship	Grass	SF	Player B	6-2, 6-4
2004	Regional League	Carpet	Final	Player A	6-3, 4-6, 6-2

Player A	Detailed analysis of last game	Player B
	Service	
58%	1st serves in	64%
86%	2nd serves in	84%
12	Aces	17
5	Double Faults	6
75%	1st serve points won	78%
55%	2nd serve points won	48%
	Returns	
64%	All returns in	58%
66%	Forehand returns in	62%
62%	Backhand returns in	54%
	Tactics	
52%	Points won at net	58%
55%	Points won from baseline	48%
	Strokes	
4	Volley winners	7
2	Smash winners	4
8	Passing winners	2
4	Lob winners	1

IMPROVING YOUR INVESTIGATION OF PERFORMANCE (INTERMEDIATE 2 LEVEL)

At Intermediate 2 level, your aim is to provide a clear and precise explanation of how you collected information (data) and why the methods used were accurate (valid). This makes it possible for you to explain your performance strengths and weaknesses and development needs.

The following stages are important:

- What you did?   ● How you did it?   ● Where you did it?
- Why you did it?

Study the example below:

Example: Volleyball with Skills and Techniques

Stage	Activity	Record and description	Notes
What you did?		I collected information on the most important skills in volleyball. These were volleying, digging, serving, spiking and blocking. I recorded my performance during a 4v4 inter-school tournament. For my first look at my performance (initial data). I recorded whether I carried out these skills effectively, with limited effectiveness or ineffectively. I then went on to take a more detailed (specific data) look at the skill of spiking. I did this because my initial data showed that spiking was my least effective skill.	Effectively links between methods of collecting information, how observation and recording will take place and the skills involved have been clearly established.
How you did it?		One of my classmates observed my performance during the inter-school tournament and collected data on my performance during the small-sided games. It was possible for them to record my performance accurately as they had to pay attention to my performance only and not to those of others in the class. This made recording possible. When observing, my classmate stood close to the half of the court I was on so that he/she could closely observe my performance. My classmate had experience of volleyball and this helped ensure that observations recorded were accurate.	Clear reference to the importance of analysing performance in meaningful contexts, i.e. small-sided games, has been mentioned
Where you did it?		The observation schedules were completed at the local sports centre where the inter-school tournament was taking place. This was a very good venue as the court was a good size for 4x4 games of volleyball. In addition there was a lot of space beside to record results.	Clear reference to where information was collected.
Why you did it?		Collecting data using observation schedules from small-sided games is a way of gaining accurate information about my strengths and weaknesses in different volleyball skills; these are all important for improving performance.	Relevant points about linking observation schedule to own strengths and weaknesses are made.

In the previous volleyball example, the initial data might look like the table below.

SKILL	Effective (✓)	Limited effectiveness (?)	Ineffective (✗)
Volley	✓✓✓✓	???	✗✗
Dig	✓✓✓	??	✗✗
Serve	✓✓✓✓✓	??	✗
Spiking	✓	??	✗✗✗✗
Blocking	✓✓✓✓	?	✗✗

IMPROVING YOUR INVESTIGATION OF PERFORMANCE (HIGHER LEVEL)

At Higher level, your aim is to analyse how you collected information (data) and why the methods used for collecting information were valid. This then makes it possible for you to analyse your performance strengths and weaknesses and development needs.

 There are many different methods of collecting information. Choose methods that will allow you to 'paint a picture' of what you did when performing. You can then provide a detailed analysis of why your methods were appropriate and valid.

You will find it useful to consider:

- the nature and demands of the activity
- your specific role and responsibilities within the activity
- your current level of performance
- the area of Analysis and Development of Performance being studied.

The purpose of collected information is to provide you with a record of your performance to which you can make further, regular references. Within your explanations, it is often important to have a balance between quantitative (objective, clearly measurable information) and qualitative (subjective, opinion-based information). Achieving this balance helps you to develop depth in your answers. Consider the following example from football where information has been collected about passing ability in a small-sided football game.

Collecting information in football

(Visual picture)	(Verbal written description)	
Football game	Objective	Subjective
	Most effective/least effective parts of your game as shown by: • number of passes completed • distance and direction of passes • degree of opposition when making passes	Your own thoughts and feelings about how well you played, e.g. • self control during game • level of confidence, anxiety, determination, motivation

In this example, the combination of objective and subjective information about methods of collecting information could add to your explanation's depth. For example, you could explain how making effective and ineffective passes affected your level of confidence throughout the game.

If your data is purely objective or subjective, it might well be less detailed. For example, through concentrating on just the facts and figures of passes you made or through only considering your thoughts and feelings (without considering the frame of reference provided by detailed passing information), parts of the whole 'picture' of your passing would be missing.

MARKED EXAMPLES OF INVESTIGATION OF PERFORMANCE (HIGHER LEVEL)

Two examples of Investigating Performance at Higher level follow. The first example is based on the SQA markers' instructions, which tell markers what to look for in good answers. The second example provides a complete model answer.

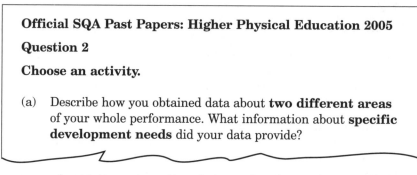

Official SQA Past Papers: Higher Physical Education 2005

Question 2

Choose an activity.

(a) Describe how you obtained data about **two different areas** of your whole performance. What information about **specific development needs** did your data provide?

Your answer should demonstrate Knowledge and Understanding in relation to one or more related methods. For example, you may have used different methods of analysis which are relevant to general and focused data. The methods selected may include qualitative or quantitative detail in relation to a selected skill or technique / fitness; general or specific, etc. The information should include a brief description and offer relevant details of associated criteria. Examples may include:

- Movement Analysis: (Observation schedule, Match Analysis sheet)
- Preparation / Action / Recovery: Mechanical Analysis of force, levers, propulsion, etc.
- Consideration of Quality: reflecting on whether your skill or technique was controlled / fluent, or fast / slow
- Video: Comparison of your performance with that of a model performer. The video allowed playback, freeze frame.
- Questionnaire: Questions should be relevant to and have responses such as 'done well', 'needs improvement' or mark your performance on a graded scale.

Your answer must include evaluative comments about what the data highlighted means in relation to the strengths and weaknesses of your performances. For example, 'a review of the video showed that I had excellent technique and ... Results from my questionnaire suggested that I am competent in the execution of my simple skills but less consistent when I perform complex skills... etc.'

Official SQA Past Papers: Higher Physical Education 2005 Specimen Question Paper

Question 2

Choose one activity.

(a)   During your course you will have gathered data about different aspects of your whole performance in this activity. Discuss the significance of the information your data generated for two different aspects of your performance.

The data methods I used included the video, match analysis sheets and specific questionnaire sheet. I wanted to find out how effective I was in my role as a wing defence in netball. Specifically, I wanted to know if I performed my defending and attacking duties consistently throughout the game. I decided to use the video as this was the best tool of analysis to avoid human error. The game is fast paced and I did not want to miss anything. The video allowed me to look at my game several times which let me check my match analysis and questionnaire sheets to see if they backed up what I was seeing. The match analysis was divided into five minute slots for each of the four quarters. I asked my marker to indicate the number of passes I made, the number of passes I tipped or intercepted, the number of times I forced my partner to commit a foul or time violation, the number of unforced errors I made. My questionnaire was designed specifically to evaluate my mental fitness. The specificity of the questions related to my success rate at controlling my temper; especially after making unforced errors or when the score was tight.

I was able to use these methods to define my strengths and weaknesses in my performance. The analysis of my data showed that I performed most of my defensive duties well. My percentages of interceptions, blocks and forced time violations were high; especially at the centre pass. I was not so consistent when performing my attacking duties, when our own GA and WA were being tightly marked. I should have been ready to get out and take this pass, instead I was slow to react to my centre requiring assistance and caused her to time violate. I was also mistiming my long feed into the circle and did not take enough notice of our opponents' GD; this meant I was throwing away potential shooting opportunities. I could see this first hand from the video action as I saw my poor ability to handle my emotions. This features as real weakness in my game and the results shown in my questionnaire reveal that on too many occasions I get caught up on poor umpire decisions, comments made by my opponents or indeed my dropped head and continual talking to myself when I make unforced errors.

4 | Analysing Performance

Introduction

Key Concepts in Analysis and Development of Performance

Improving your Analysis of Performance

Marked examples of Analysis of Performance (Higher level)

INTRODUCTION

After you have investigated your performance and collected valid information the second step is to effectively analyse your performance. This is critical for developing your understanding. The key requirement is to link **'what you did'** when collecting information to **'why it is important'** for analysing performance.

 Example: Volleyball with Skills and Techniques

Recall

...what you did   ...how you did it   ...where you did it   ...why you did it

Report 'Why was it important?'

In your writing, try to move beyond stating established facts to discussing why these facts were important. For example, when writing about principles of training, try to move beyond writing about what specificity and progressive overload are to discussing how you applied **your understanding** of principles of training in the development of your performance. This will help to develop the content of your answers while still being based on your performance experience, (see example below).

> It was important that I collected information from my whole performance because this gave me a genuine overall view of my strengths and weaknesses. I needed to know how effective my performance was in a game, as opposed to in practice, because this is a better indicator of my true ability. This was my first priority. The collected information showed that my spiking required a more detailed analysis.
>
> Next, I needed to look at methods of collecting information that were both reliable and valid (accurate) for assessing my performance in a volleyball game. I decided that observation schedules would be a useful method, because they would enable analysis of my performance in small-sided volleyball games. I collected some initial information that established whether my skills were effective, of limited effectiveness or ineffective. After this, I made a detailed, specific analysis of my spiking. This analysis broke the skill down into Preparation/Action/Recovery. This allowed a more detailed assessment of my weaknesses.
>
> This method of collecting information (observation schedules) was a suitable method because it was possible for a classmate who had a good level of experience and expertise in volleyball to accurately record my performance.

	Clear reference to the importance of analysing performance in meaningful contexts.
	Effective links between methods of collecting information, how observation and recording will take place and the skills involved have been established.

Note: The answer is written in the 'first person' ('I did…'). This is important because **your** experience is the basis of your answer.

 When completing your Unit Assessment in the Analysis and Development of Performance Unit you are required to link your answer to **two** Key Concepts. Understanding which two Key Concepts you are focusing on is important. So, check that you are familiar with the Key Concepts in the different areas of Analysis and Development of Performance.

KEY CONCEPTS IN ANALYSIS AND DEVELOPMENT OF PERFORMANCE

Performance Appreciation (Area 1)

is a **general** broad view of performance which relates to the three other specific areas of analysis of performance.

Key Concepts

- The overall nature and demands of quality performance.
- Technical, physical, personal and special qualities of performance.
- Mental factors influencing performance.
- The use of appropriate models of performance.
- Planning and managing personal performance improvement.

Preparation of the Body (Area 2)

is a **specific** analysis of the fitness and training requirements necessary for your performance.

Key Concepts

- Fitness assessment in relation to personal performance and the demands of activities.
- Application of different types of fitness in the development of activity specific performance.
- Physical, skill-related and mental aspects of fitness.
- Principles and methods of training.
- Planning, implementing and monitoring training.

Skills and Techniques (Area 3)

is a **specific** analysis of your skills and techniques needs in performance.

Key Concepts

- The concepts of skill and skilled performance.
- Skill / technique improvement through mechanical analysis or movement analysis or consideration of quality.
- The development of skill and the refinement of technique.

Structures, Strategies and Composition (Area 4)

is a **specific** analysis of the influence of shape, form and design on your performance.

Key Concepts

- The structures, strategies and / or compositional elements that are fundamental to activities.
- Identification of strengths and weaknesses in performance in terms of: roles and relationships, formations, tactical or design elements, choreography and composition.
- Information processing, problem-solving and decision-making when working to develop and improve performance.

IMPROVING YOUR ANALYSIS OF PERFORMANCE

Linking methods of collecting information to Analysis of Performance

 Here are four examples of how methods of collecting information link to each of the areas of Analysis and Development of Performance. They are:

Activities	Area of Analysis and Development of Performance	Method of collecting information	Key Concept
Basketball	Performance Appreciation	Questionnaire	Technical, physical, personal and special qualities of performance
Athletics	Preparation of the Body	Knowledge of results	Fitness assessment in relation to personal performance and the demands of activities
Football – Tackling	Skills and Techniques	Observation schedule	Skill / technique improvement through mechanical analysis or movement analysis or consideration of quality
Football – Retaining possession	Structures, Strategies and Composition	Game analysis	Identification of strengths and weaknesses in performance in terms of: roles and relationships, formations, tactical or design elements, choreography and composition

Excellent answers establish clear feasible links between activities, the area of Analysis and Development of Performance, methods of collecting information and Key Concepts. Ensure you establish and understand the links in your course. Note how the same activity can be used as the basis for analysis in different areas of Analysis and Development of Performance. Four examples are now provided.

Example 1: Performance Appreciation / Basketball team responsibilities (forward)

Area of Analysis and Development of Performance	Method of collecting information	Key Concept
Performance Appreciation	Questionnaire	Technical, physical, personal and special qualities of performance

Questionnaire

<u>Technical qualities of performance</u>
- How effective was my passing, dribbling and shooting in attack?
- How effective was my marking in defence? Was I able to prevent attackers cutting to the basket? How many fouls did I commit?

<u>Physical qualities of performance</u>
- Was I able to sustain my performance throughout the whole game through having good cardiorespiratory endurance?
- Was I powerful when driving to the basket and rebounding?

<u>Personal qualities of performance</u>
- Did I manage to control my emotions throughout the game?
- Was I determined when driving to the basket?

<u>Special qualities of performance</u>
- Was I able to surprise the marking defenders with the attacking options I selected?
- Was I able to perform to the best of my ability in front of spectators?

Example 2: Preparation of the Body / Athletics – 1500 m

Area of Analysis and Development of Performance	Method of collecting information	Key Concept
Preparation of the Body	Knowledge of results	Fitness assessment in relation to personal performance and the demands of activities

Knowledge of results

Understanding of the 12-minute Cooper Test procedure for collecting information will help you to compare your performance data to class and national norms for different ages and for male and female students in long distance running events. Fitness assessments during and at the end of a training programme can provide relevant information for comparison.

12-minute Cooper Test

Aim   To calculate your level of cardiorespiratory endurance by applying a time / distance formula

Equipment   A flat area, e.g. outdoor field or athletics track

Test Procedure   12 minutes to cover the maximum distance possible through running, jogging or walking

Test Calculation   Use the table below to measure your own performance

Performer		Performance level			
Age	Sex	Excellent	Good	Fair	Poor
13–14 years	male	2700	2400	2200	2100
	female	2000	1900	1600	1500
15–16 years	male	2800	2500	2300	2200
	female	2100	1900	1700	1500
17–18 years	male	3000	2700	2500	2300
	female	2300	2100	1800	1500

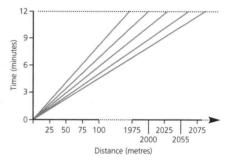

Example 3: Skills and Techniques / Football (Midfielder / Tackling)

Area of Analysis and Development of Performance	Method of collecting information	Key Concept
Skills and Techniques	Observation schedule	Skill/technique improvement through mechanical analysis or movement analysis or consideration of quality

Observation schedule

When making a detailed plan for completing an analysis of your technique, you need to consider the criteria you would use for analysing the development of your performance.

Your analysis of a football tackle could, for example, focus on any of the different types of analysis outlined in the following observation schedules.

SCOTSTOWN ACADEMY
Intermediate 2 and Higher Level P.E. – Observation Schedule
Technique Analysis to identify Strengths/Weaknesses

Date: _____ Venue: _____ Assessor: _____

MECHANICAL ANALY

SKILL: _Tackling_   TECHNIQUE

Essential Features	Model Performer	Sel Date
Centre of Gravity		
Force		
Resistance		

CRITERIA TO BE USED FOR ASSES
✓ = highly effective – fluent, co
? = limited effectiveness – need
✗ = ineffective – needs conside

Your mechanical analysis could focus on: use of centre of gravity, force and resistance.

SCOTSTOWN ACADEMY
Intermediate 2 and Higher Level P.E. – Observation Schedule
Technique Analysis to identify Strengths/Weaknesses

Date: _____ Venue: _____ Assessor: _____

MOVEMENT ANALYS

SKILL: _Tackling_   TECHNIQUE:

Essential Features	Model Performer	Self Date 1
Preparation		
Action		
Recovery		

CRITERIA TO BE USED FOR ASSESS
✓ = highly effective – fluent, cont
? = limited effectiveness – needs
✗ = ineffective – needs considera

Your movement analysis could focus on: Preparation / Action / Recovery.

SCOTSTOWN ACADEMY
Intermediate 2 and Higher Level P.E. – Observation Schedule
Technique Analysis to identify Strengths/Weaknesses

Date: _____ Venue: _____ Assessor: _____ Role: _____

CONSIDERATION OF QUALITY

SKILL: _Tackling_   TECHNIQUE: _Side Tackle_

Essential Features	Model Performer	Self Date 1	Self Date 2	Additional Comments
Physical				
Personal				
Special				

CRITERIA TO BE USED FOR ASSESSING PERFORMANCE
✓ = highly effective – fluent, controlled, etc.
? = limited effectiveness – needs improvement
✗ = ineffective – needs considerable improvement

Your consideration of quality could focus on: physical (e.g. strength), personal (e.g. determination) and special (e.g. being able to adapt and switch to tackle opponents in most dangerous positions).

Collecting data in this way will provide you with valuable information. Even within specified approaches, such as movement analysis, you may consider that a different type of information is necessary to help improve your performance.

When you are completing your detailed plan for analysing technique it is important that you continually review and monitor improvements. The observation schedules above enable this to occur. After comparing yourself to a model performer at the outset (Self date 1) a further reassessment is possible (Self date 2) so that review and monitoring of progress is possible. Further review of progress opportunities could be added as necessary. Monitoring ongoing analysis of performance improvements would be important whenever using mechanical analysis, movement analysis or consideration of quality.

Example 4: Structures, Strategies and Composition / Football

Area of Analysis and Development of Performance	Method of collecting information	Key Concept
Structures, Strategies and Composition	Game analysis	Identification of strengths and weaknesses in performance in terms of: roles and relationships, formations, tactical or design elements, choreography and composition

Game analysis

Effective game analysis requires accurate observation and recall. Video of performance is often used to help recall important details about a game. In order to make sure analysis is objective and based on accurate and reliable details game analysis is often used by performers and teachers.

Game analysis can be used to identify and measure a range of performance indicators such as the effectiveness of an overall strategy as well as individual player analysis. In the following example, the intention is to understand more about the effectiveness of how well a striker in football retains possession of the ball when playing as one of two strikers in a 3-5-2 formation. Data is collected from the passes received in the attacking third of the pitch.

Team: _Scotstown Academy_   Role: _Attacker_   Opposition: _Central High School_   Date: _5/11/06_

Game analysis – Check 1 – Possession won or lost?
Retained possession 12 – lost possession 8

Game analysis – Check 2 – How was possession won?
Held the ball and passed to midfield players on five occasions
Held the ball and passed to attacking players on three occasions
Played one touch pass on two occasions
Turned defender and shot on goal twice. scoring one goal

Game analysis – Check 3 – How was possession lost?
Retained posession but pass was intercepted on four occasions
Was tackled by defender on three occasions
Had attempted first time pass intercepted on one occasion

MARKED EXAMPLES OF ANALYSIS OF PERFORMANCE (HIGHER LEVEL)

Two marked examples of Analysing Performance at Higher level follow. The first example is based on the SQA markers' instructions, which tell markers what to look for in good answers. The second example provides a complete model answer.

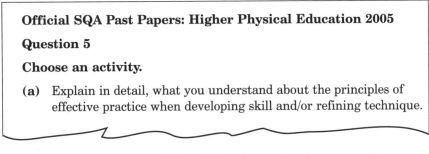

Official SQA Past Papers: Higher Physical Education 2005

Question 5

Choose an activity.

(a) Explain in detail, what you understand about the principles of effective practice when developing skill and/or refining technique.

Your answer should show knowledge of the relevant Key Concept and its application. This addresses the ways of learning skills and developing technique.

Your responses should reflect that practice methods selected for improvement should be specific to complexity of skill and relevant to your stage of learning. The acronym SMARTER. is useful for this purpose. For example, practice should be specific, measurable, attainable, realistic, time related, exciting and regular. Other relevant knowledge will reference factors such as practice needs to show progression to ensure targets were reached / enabled refinement / remediation / regression as required, increased motivation, improved confidence, consideration of work-rest ratio, etc.

Official SQA Past Papers: Higher Physical Education 2005

Question 6

(c) From the list below, select two of the factors that are influential in skill development. Discuss how each of the factors chosen affected the development of your skill or technique during practice.
- motivation
- feedback
- anxiety
- concentration
- confidence

The two factors that affected the development of my vaulting ability were feedback and confidence. When practising my first vault I relied very much on kinaesthetic feedback. I was already comfortable with the skill and so could feel how well I was performing. I knew when my legs were not extended or whether I had managed to spot my landings accurately or not. I also received verbal and visual external feedback from my coach, which also helped me to improve the overall quality of my technique. As the feedback was immediate I was able to take on the advice given and put it back into my whole performance. This type of feedback was important but had more of an impact on me as I practised my second vault. This was because this vault was much harder to perform. There were more sub-sections involved and therefore I needed diagnostic feedback from my coach to enable me to refine specific parts of my vault. I also needed the feedback frequently as I was not consistent and made errors at different sections.

Closely related to feedback was my confidence. Due to the danger element of performing vaults it was crucial to be confident in myself so that I would not tense up and mistime my run up or take off. I had to be confident in my 'spotters' who were there to prevent me from falling. The repetitive nature of my practice increased my confidence very quickly and so I was able to make my performance look very relaxed and easy to perform. The gradual build up process reinforced my inner confidence, the more feedback I got the more confident I became and the fear of falling became less of an issue. My confidence also affected the aesthetic impression of my vault in that when I was unafraid I was able to get much higher in my flight phase and could also rotate more quickly on my half-twist dismount. During competition my confidence had to be exceptionally positive so that I would not make mistakes. At this time although I was nervous because I was performing in front of a crowd, I had to ensure I believed in myself and so make my vaults look more spectacular and so gain higher points from the judges.

5 Developing Performance

Introduction

Improving your Development of Performance

Marked examples of Development of Performance (Higher level)

INTRODUCTION

Developing performance is the third key step in the Cycle of Analysis. After you have collected information about your performance and related this to selected Key Concepts, the next requirement is to explain how you developed your performance.

In developing your performance you should try to regularly monitor and review your performance. The more continuously you check on your progress the better prepared you will be to make any necessary adaptations to your training programme. Link your planned performance improvements to your short- and long-term goals. Use feedback you gain from monitoring your performance to revise your goals as necessary.

When monitoring your performance you should try to refer to the data you have collected about your performance as often as possible. This will provide you with accurate information to help you make comparisons with your more recent performances.

> Try to ensure that your suggested improvements build upon the data you have collected and your understanding of relevant Key Concepts.

IMPROVING YOUR DEVELOPMENT OF PERFORMANCE

Example 1 (continued): Performance Appreciation / Basketball team responsibilities (forward)

Now that you have collected information about your performance and understand in greater detail different **qualities involved in performance**, the next step is to develop your performance programme. This involves defining your **plan of action, setting goals** and **monitoring performance**. Overall, your answer requires to be detailed and show critical thinking.

Recap:

Step 1: Investigate Performance: Collecting information about performance (Questionnaire) ✔

Step 2: Analyse Performance: Underpinning knowledge about Key Concept – Technical, physical, personal and special qualities of performance ✔

Review: Personal qualities of performance

- Did I manage to control my emotions throughout the game?
- Was I determined when driving to the basket?

Next step: Develop Performance

Establish links with relevant Key Concepts for Developing Performance. In this example:

- Planning and managing personal performance improvement

Plan of action

- Your plan of action could explain how training is game-like and links to your role as a forward in basketball.

- Further details could expand upon how your plan links to your responsibilities for defending as part of a team unit in defence and for shooting and rebounding in attack.

- This might lead to the development of small practice games which focus on **managing and controlling your emotions** in defence and **determination** when driving to the basket in attack. Here you would show that you understood how relevant practice considerations could be applied to your performance. For example, the opposing team could deliberately set up attacks against your side of the defence and you could practise driving to the basket under full game conditions.

- You could then explain how you anticipate that improvements from practice games will help you have greater control of your emotions and more determination in full games.

 When designing a training programme it is useful to set performance goals. The 'SMARTER' acronym is often useful for checking that there are clear links between your goals and the programme that you are following to improve performance.

S	Specific	Developed small practice games which focused on managing and controlling emotions in defence and determination when driving to the basket in attack.	✔
M	Measurable	Regularly reviewed performance against questionnaire data.	✔
A	Agreed	Checked practice training plan over with teacher.	✔
R	Realistic	Game-like practices ensured practices linked to real game situations.	✔
T	Time-phased	Ensured that short-term goal of increasing control in performance was achieved before longer term training goals were set.	✔
E	Exciting	Practice with team mates made it exciting and avoided any boredom affecting training.	✔
R	Recorded	Linked training programmes to relevant methods of recording information	✔

Monitoring performance

- To monitor your performance you need to review how your personal qualities in performance (managing emotions and determination) have improved.

- You can do this by reflecting upon your performance and reassessing your performance by asking yourself again the general questions which formed your initial investigation of performance.

- You could also ask yourself more specific performance questions such as when defending were you able to block out distractions, appear relaxed, avoid negative thoughts when the opposing team scored and take in information from team mates about moving as part of a defensive unit.

- When driving to the basket in attack were you determined throughout the game not to make any unforced errors?

- Were you able to cope with any physical contact which can occur if opposing players commit a foul?

Example 2 (continued): Preparation of the Body / Athletics – 1500 m

Now that you have **knowledge of your results** about your performance from a well-known and valid **fitness test**, with which you can compare your performance data to class and national norms for different ages and for male and female students in long-distance running events, the next step is to develop your performance programme. This involves defining your plan of action, setting goals and monitoring performance. Overall, your answer requires to be detailed and show critical thinking.

Recap:

Step 1: Investigate Performance: Collecting information about performance (Knowledge of results) ✔

Step 2: Analyse Performance: Underpinning knowledge about Key Concept – Fitness assessment in relation to personal performance and the demands of activities ✔

Review: Fitness assessment

● How do my test scores compare with female students of a similar age?

● How do my test results categorise my performance – Excellent, Good, Fair or Poor?

Next step: Develop Performance

Establish links with relevant Key Concepts for Developing Performance. In this example:

● Principles and methods of training

Plan of action

● Your plan of action could explain the benefits of progressively overloading your training in athletics through applying the principle of specificity.

● Further details could then expand upon how the principles of training link to your specialist running event (1500 m), for example, through explaining how you adapt progressive overload during training.

● This might lead to the development of your explanation about methods of training. For example, fartlek training based on continuous running as well as short sprint bursts. You would explain how the benefits of fartlek training could be applied to your specific performance. For example, that you require both aerobic (continuous running) as well as anaerobic (short speed sprints) to match the demands of the 1500 m.

When designing a training programme it is useful to set performance goals. This could happen by explaining the level of improvement expected following a period of physical fitness training.

- You could explain overall race times, for example, that you expect to move from your current time of 6 m 10 secs to a time under 6 m and closer to 5 m 45 secs.

- You could also explain your performance goals for particular parts of the1500 m race as well, for example, that your last lap (400 m) target time was now 1 m 20 secs instead of 1 m 30 secs.

Monitoring performance

- To monitor your performance you need to review how effectively you progressively overloaded your training through analysis of the fartlek programme you developed.

- You could review how effective your methods of training were. Was your training challenging yet realistic, well organised and suitable for your performance needs?

- This involves explaining any adaptations made to the programme as it progressed, or why you left the programme unchanged.

- You can reassess your performance by completing further 12-minute Cooper Tests which formed your initial investigation of performance.

Example 3 (continued): Skills and Techniques / Football (Midfielder / Tackling)

Now that you have completed an observation schedule, which has analysed your side tackling technique by a **movement analysis** comparison of your **preparation, action and recovery** with that of a model performer, the next step is to develop your performance programme. This involves defining your plan of action, setting goals and monitoring performance. Overall, your answer requires to be detailed and show critical thinking.

Recap:

Step 1: Investigate Performance: Collecting information about performance (Observation schedule) ✔

Step 2: Analyse Performance: Underpinning knowledge about Key Concept – Skill / technique improvement through mechanical analysis or movement analysis or consideration of quality ✔

Understanding of the different types of skill / technique analysis possible – mechanical, movement and consideration of quality – will help you to develop the skill of tackling and to refine the technique of the side tackle specifically.

Review: Skills and Techniques assessment

● How does my tackling compare with that of a model performer?
● What are my areas of strength and weakness?
● Which area of my tackling requires the greatest improvement – preparation, action or recovery?

Next step: Develop Performance

Establish links with relevant Key Concepts for Developing Performance. In this example:

● The development of skill and the refinement of technique

Plan of action

● Your plan of action could begin by explaining the stage of skill learning of your tackling ability.

- Next, you could explain the practice methods which were best for improving your tackling technique. For example, that a mix of repetition and drills practices which are evaluated through small conditioned games were considered the best methods of practice for your performance needs.

- This explanation should demonstrate that you understand relevant principles of effective practice.

- This might lead to the development of your explanation about the importance of concentration when defending and tackling as a midfield player in football.

 When designing a training programme it is useful to set performance goals. This could happen by explaining the level of improvement expected following a skills and techniques based training programme.

- You could explain how specific improvements to preparation, action and recovery parts of your tackling could ensure your performance was more effective through, for example, winning possession more often, committing fewer fouls, forcing opposing players to move away to less attacking parts of the pitch.

Monitoring performance

- To monitor your performance you need to review the effectiveness of your skills and techniques based training programme.

- You could review how effective your methods of training were. Was your training challenging yet realistic, well organised and suitable for your performance needs?

- You could also evaluate your level of concentration during the drills and conditioned games.

Example 4 (continued): Structures, Strategies and Composition / Football

Now that you have completed a game analysis, which has analysed your ability to retain possession of the ball as part of your involvement in a 3-5-2 formation in football, the next step is to develop your performance programme. This involves defining your plan of action, setting goals and monitoring performance. Overall, your answer requires to be detailed and show critical thinking.

Recap:

Step 1: Investigate Performance: Collecting information about performance (Game analysis) ✔

Step 2: Analyse Performance: Underpinning knowledge about Key Concept – Identification of strengths and weaknesses in performance in terms of: roles and relationships, formations, tactical or design elements, choreography and composition ✔

Understanding of different types of football formations and how they can be adapted to make them more effective will help you make decisions about how you and your team can work together to retain possession of the ball when attacking.

Review: Structures, strategies and composition assessment

● How effective is retention of possession at present?

● How is possession won at present and how is it lost?

● Which area of securing possession requires greatest improvement?

Next step: Develop Performance

Establish links with relevant Key Concepts for Developing Performance. In this example:

● Information processing, problem-solving and decision-making when working to develop and improve performance

Plan of action

● Your plan of action could begin by explaining how you intend to improve your attacking options through better problem-solving and decision-making.

- Next, you could explain the variables which appear to affect winning and securing possession in attacking positions, for example, effective communication between players, greater support from midfield players, attempting to 'drop off' into midfield to make it easier to receive a pass.
- This explanation should demonstrate that you understand relevant principles of play – width, depth, mobility.
- This might lead to the development of your explanation about the importance of refining and adapting your formation in football in order to increase attacking options.

 When designing a training programme it is useful to set performance goals. This could happen by explaining the level of improvement expected following refinements and adaptations to your formation in football when attacking.

- You could explain how specific improvements in your formation were expected to result in fewer instances of passes being intercepted, of being caught in possession, or tackled by defenders.

Monitoring performance

- To monitor your performance you need to review the effectiveness of your strategy of using the 3-5-2 formation in football and the benefits it had for width, depth and mobility.
- As part of this review, you could monitor how effectively you carried out your attacking role, where a major area of responsibility was to secure possession and involve other team mates in creating goal scoring opportunities.
- Overall, were the refinements and adaptations to your formation suitable for your team?

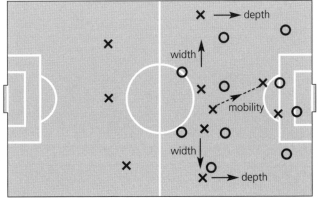

MARKED EXAMPLES OF DEVELOPMENT OF PERFORMANCE (HIGHER LEVEL)

Two marked examples of Developing Performance at Higher level follow. The first example is based on the SQA markers' instructions, which tell markers what to look for in good answers. The second example provides a complete model answer.

Official SQA Past Papers: Higher Physical Education 2005

5. (c) Describe, in detail, a programme of work you used to develop this skill or technique. Give examples of how the principles of practice were applied in the programme.

Your depth of response must be detailed and demonstrate critical thinking. You must show evidence of how the selected methods of practice featured as important aspects within your programme. This should be relevant to your identified skills or techniques / complexity of the task / stages of learning, etc. As you offer detailed explanation about your programme you must show how you applied the principles of practice to ensure your programme was successful. For example, 'I made my problem-solving drills game-like so that I would be challenged and motivated to succeed ... I made my practice harder by adding in more defenders ... I got immediate feedback on my performance so that I knew when I had improved ... Once I had reached my target I would use more complex drills such as ... To ensure I did not become bored I decided to... etc.'

Official SQA Past Papers: Higher Physical Education 2005 – Specimen Question Paper

6 (d)   Describe in detail, how you monitored your progress during practice. Explain what you did to ensure your progress was continuous.

I used several methods to monitor my progress during practice. Firstly I used my initial target drill percentages to allow me to make comparisons. During my training I could see which of the techniques – topspin, slice or flat – I had more success with. I could also tell whether I was better on the right or left hand side of the court and also relied on my kinaesthetic feedback as I developed a better sense of 'knowing' when I had hit a good serve. I could feel and see improvements, for example, when I felt I had placed a wide and deep topspin serve I knew to quickly follow in and finish the rally with a strong punch volley – this was happening more frequently.

I also filmed my performance during practice and match sessions to let me see first hand how I looked and where on the court I favoured placement. I could also rewind this and get feedback on errors featuring as problems on any of the subroutines of my action. Part of my monitoring process was to talk over with my coach what I saw when we replayed the tape. I found this motivating as my coach encouraged me to vary the serve and take in more of the game cues such as positioning of my opponent on court and so learn to adjust and vary my serve selection more effectively. The most obvious indicator was my match statistics. By comparing my previous game stats I was able to examine first serves won, double fault errors and percentage serve placements, etc. I used all of these methods to help me to plan appropriate practice and ensure I progressed. I highlighted areas of weakness and could use regulated court practice to ensure I got more ace serves in and so win games in three sets rather than being pushed into a punishing five setter.

6 Reviewing / Evaluating Performance

INTRODUCTION

Ensure that your review of performance includes both specific and general aspects of performance. For example, if you are trying to improve serving in table tennis then review both the effectiveness of your serving in table tennis and the effect it has on your overall table tennis game. In discussing your performance improvements try to link them to the performance abilities which are required within the Performance Unit.

> Try to relate performance improvement to the repertoire of skills and techniques required, effective decision-making and control and fluency. If you can make these performance connections it will help add to the depth and quality of performance review.

IMPROVING YOUR REVIEWING AND EVALUATION OF PERFORMANCE

 Example 1 (continued): Performance Appreciation / Basketball team responsibilities (forward)

Recap:

Step 1: Investigate Performance: Collecting information about performance (Questionnaire) ✔

Step 2: Analyse Performance: Underpinning knowledge about Key Concept – Technical, physical, personal and special qualities of performance ✔

Step 3: Develop Performance ✔
Plan of action – Small practice games focusing on managing and controlling your emotions in defence and determination when driving to the basket in attack
Setting goals – Apply 'SMARTER' acronym for goal setting
Monitoring performance – Review how your personal qualities in performance (managing emotions and determination) have improved

Step 4: **Review / Evaluate Performance**

- The key to success is to link your forward responsibilities in basketball to your ability to manage your emotions and show determination in whole games of basketball.

- In doing this you link the three critical parts of an effective evaluation together, namely, your performance abilities, your underpinning knowledge of Key Concepts in performance appreciation and the nature and demands of the game of basketball.

Example 2 (continued): Preparation of the Body / Athletics – 1500 m

Recap:

Step 1: Investigate Performance: Collecting information about performance (Knowledge of results)   ✔

Step 2: Analyse Performance: Underpinning knowledge about Key Concept – Fitness assessment in relation to personal performance and the demands of activities   ✔

Step 3: Develop Performance: ✔
Plan of action – Apply principles and methods of training understanding to develop fartlek training programme based on continuous running as well as short sprint bursts
Setting goals – Explain your performance goals for particular parts of the1500 m race as well for the whole race
Monitoring performance – Evaluate how effective your training programme was in terms of your performance needs

Step 4: **Review / Evaluate Performance**

● The key to success is to link your ability at running 1500 m races with your ability to apply your understanding principles and methods of training in the context of middle distance track events in athletics.

● In doing this you link the three critical parts of an effective evaluation together, namely, your performance abilities, your underpinning knowledge of Key Concepts in preparation of the body and the nature and demands of middle distance track events in athletics.

Example 3 (continued): Skills and Techniques / Football (Midfielder / Tackling)

Recap:

Step 1: Investigate Performance: Collecting information about performance (Observation schedule) ✔

Step 2: Analyse Performance: Underpinning knowledge about Key Concept – Skill / technique improvement through mechanical analysis or movement analysis or consideration of quality ✔

Step 3: Develop Performance: ✔
Plan of action – Devise a skills-based training programme of repetition and drills practices
Setting goals – Define performance goals for each part of side tackling (preparation, action and recovery)
Monitoring performance – Evaluate how effective your training programme was in terms of your tackling in football

Step 4: **Review / Evaluate Performance**

- The key to success is to link your ability at tackling in football with your ability to apply your understanding of principles of effective and practice methods in the context of football.

- In doing this you link the three critical parts of an effective evaluation together, namely, your performance abilities, your underpinning knowledge of Key Concepts in skills and techniques and the nature and demands of competitive football games.

Example 4 (continued): Structures, Strategies and Composition / Football

Recap:

Step 1: Investigate Performance: Collecting information about performance (Game analysis) ✔

Step 2: Analyse Performance: Underpinning knowledge about Key Concept – Identification of strengths and weaknesses in performance in terms of: roles and relationships, formations, tactical or design elements, choreography and composition ✔

Step 3: Develop Performance: ✔
Plan of action – Apply the principles of play to your 3-5-2 formation when attacking by better practical problem solving and decision-making
Setting goals – Define performance goals about the types of refinements and adaptations expected for your formation
Monitoring performance – Evaluate how effective your training programme was in terms of improving your attacking options in football with regard to the principles of play – width, depth and mobility.

Step 4: **Review / Evaluate Performance**

- The key to success is to link your individual and team abilities at refining and adapting your 3-5-2 attacking strategy with your ability to apply your understanding of problem-solving and decision-making in football.

- In doing this you link the three critical parts of an effective evaluation together, namely, you and your team's performance abilities, your underpinning knowledge of Key Concepts in structures, strategies and composition and the nature and demands of competitive football games.

MARKED EXAMPLES OF EVALUATION OF PERFORMANCE (HIGHER LEVEL)

Two marked examples of Evaluating Performance at Higher level follow. The first example is based on the SQA markers' instructions, which tell markers what to look for in good answers. The second example provides a complete model answer.

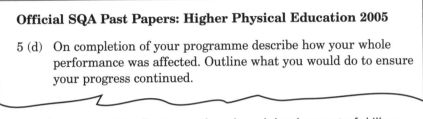

Official SQA Past Papers: Higher Physical Education 2005

5 (d)   On completion of your programme describe how your whole performance was affected. Outline what you would do to ensure your progress continued.

The depth of response will reflect upon the selected development of skill or technique. You must show critical thinking and offer evaluative comments about improved performance. This must be supported with relevant information about how your whole performance was affected. For example, 'On completion of my training I could see that I more consistently won games... The execution of my smash was much more fluent and had more power... I could now... etc. To ensure that my progress continued I would set higher targets by... I would continue to use pressure drills but add in ... I would compare my results and, if required, go back and further refine my technique by... etc.'

Official SQA Past Papers: Higher Physical Education 2005

3 (d)   Discuss the effects that your training had on your whole performance.

When I was playing games I noticed that I was able to sustain a higher and more consistent skill level for longer because of my improved CRE. I was able to maintain my performance for longer and the onset of fatigue in the game did not occur until much later than it previously had. This meant that I played better for longer and that I was in better condition towards the end of the game. When attacking I noticed I was still managing to support my team mates when setting up the play either with the fast break or, if this broke down, by being available to pass or shoot even in the later stages of the game. I also felt I was more able to dribble past my opponent more and, because I felt fitter and was able to keep going for longer without feeling as tired, I felt more confident in myself. Also, when defending, I felt that I was able to stay with the player I was marking and was able to get back to defend quicker if we were playing zone defence. This led to more pressure on the opposition, forcing them into mistakes which often resulted in us regaining possession and allowing my team an opportunity to score. Finally, because I felt fitter, I was motivated and happier with my performance and this improved my self confidence and led to a better overall performance.

Recap:

7 Improving Your Cycle of Analysis Study

Introduction

Improving your Cycle of Analysis study

Cycles of Analysis study

INTRODUCTION

As you progress through your course the intention is that you can link your understanding of the investigative process to your understanding of the content knowledge within the Key Concepts.

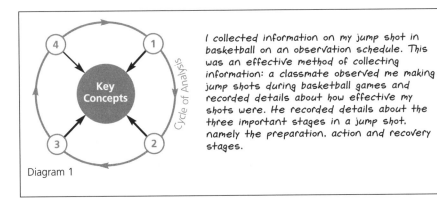

I collected information on my jump shot in basketball on an observation schedule. This was an effective method of collecting information: a classmate observed me making jump shots during basketball games and recorded details about how effective my shots were. He recorded details about the three important stages in a jump shot, namely the preparation, action and recovery stages.

Diagram 1

Diagram 1 represents a student who has a clear grasp of Analysis of Performance processes (the wheel's rim) and who has successfully linked his or her answer to some relevant details within the Key Concepts (the wheel's hub).

In addition, depth in your answers can be added by ensuring that you are familiar with content detail. Diagram 2 represents how this can be achieved.

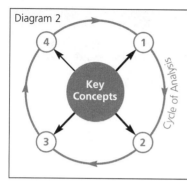

Diagram 2

It is important that any information I collected on my performance was specific to me. This was achieved through considering my level of ability, my level of fitness and, because I am in a team, my specific role. As a point guard in basketball, I often take jump shots. This is because I play around the outside of the key, quite far away from the basket. However, if a good shooting opportunity occurs, I will often take it on if this is a good option for my team.

IMPROVING YOUR CYCLE OF ANALYSIS STUDY

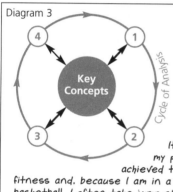

Diagram 3

I collected information on my jump shot in basketball on an observation schedule. This was an effective method of collecting information: a classmate observed me making jump shots during basketball games and recorded details about how effective my shots were. He recorded details about the three important stages in a jump shot, namely the preparation, action and recovery stages.

It is important that any information I collected on my performance was specific to me. This was achieved through considering my level of ability, my level of fitness and, because I am in a team, my specific role. As a point guard in basketball, I often take jump shots. This is because I play around the outside of the key, quite far away from the basket. However, if a good shooting opportunity occurs, I will often take it on if this is a good option for my team.

Diagram 2 represents a student who has detailed knowledge of the Key Concepts (wheel hub) as well as some relevant understanding of the relevant Analysis of Performance processes involved (wheel rim).

Diagram 3 represents the ideal – a student who understands the importance of the relevant Analysis of Performance process and the importance of relevant content knowledge equally. Aim for success by combining the two in your answers and link your practical experience and content knowledge together through the spokes in a wheel. As you move round the Cycle of Analysis (the wheel's rim) you make links with the Key Concepts (the wheel's hub) that are important in the development of your Performance, as shown by the double-headed arrows.

By merging the investigative process to your understanding of the content knowledge within the Key Concepts you are best placed to overtake the outcomes of the Analysis and Development of Performance Unit Assessment. Diagram 4 highlights how this process occurs.

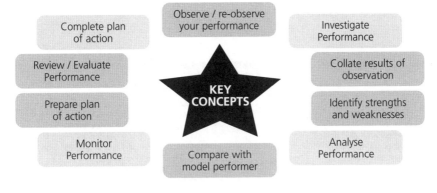

CYCLES OF ANALYSIS STUDY

Recap (see page 14):

Once you are embarked on the process of investigating and analysing performance you tend to use ongoing Cycles of Analysis. This is in order to help you develop and review / evaluate your performance in realistic ways. For example, progressing once around the Cycle of Analysis in a 30-hour block might be a little dull and lead to you make little apparent progress. By contrast, regularly monitoring and evaluating your performance allows you to build ongoing improvements and to make consistent progress.

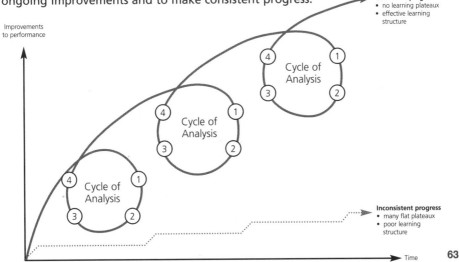

Swimming and Preparation of the Body example

A continuous Cycle of Analysis to cover a 30-hour learning and assessment plan

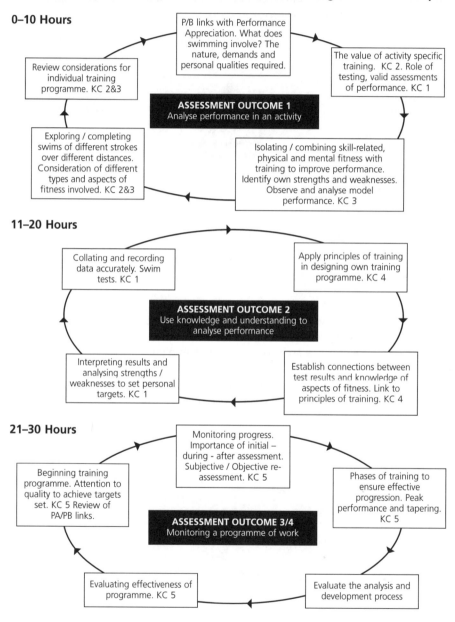

0–10 Hours

P/B links with Performance Appreciation. What does swimming involve? The nature, demands and personal qualities required.

The value of activity specific training. KC 2. Role of testing, valid assessments of performance. KC 1

Review considerations for individual training programme. KC 2&3

ASSESSMENT OUTCOME 1
Analyse performance in an activity

Exploring / completing swims of different strokes over different distances. Consideration of different types and aspects of fitness involved. KC 2&3

Isolating / combining skill-related, physical and mental fitness with training to improve performance. Identify own strengths and weaknesses. Observe and analyse model performance. KC 3

11–20 Hours

Collating and recording data accurately. Swim tests. KC 1

Apply principles of training in designing own training programme. KC 4

ASSESSMENT OUTCOME 2
Use knowledge and understanding to analyse performance

Interpreting results and analysing strengths / weaknesses to set personal targets. KC 1

Establish connections between test results and knowledge of aspects of fitness. Link to principles of training. KC 4

21–30 Hours

Monitoring progress. Importance of initial – during - after assessment. Subjective / Objective re-assessment. KC 5

Beginning training programme. Attention to quality to achieve targets set. KC 5 Review of PA/PB links.

Phases of training to ensure effective progression. Peak performance and tapering. KC 5

ASSESSMENT OUTCOME 3/4
Monitoring a programme of work

Evaluating effectiveness of programme. KC 5

Evaluate the analysis and development process

8   Assessment Preparation

Developing individual answers

How are you assessed?

Unit and Course Assessment process

Course Assessment, examples of questions, wording of questions

Improving your writing skills

DEVELOPING INDIVIDUAL ANSWERS

You may find that answering questions in Physical Education is different from answering questions in other subjects. This is because there is no single correct answer to any PE question. For example, in Higher level Mathematics, you try to work out definite correct answers. However, your answers in PE will be unique to you. This can make answering questions appear difficult to begin with. However, with practice and a clear understanding of what is being asked for, you can achieve success. This section will help you by providing you with detailed advice about how to develop your answers for both Unit and Course Assessments.

HOW ARE YOU ASSESSED?

You will be assessed both during the year (Unit Assessment) and at the end of the year (Course Assessment). You will be required to complete the following Outcomes and Performance Criteria (PCs):

Performance

For Performance, there is one Outcome. It is to:

'demonstrate effective performance in challenging contexts'.

Whichever activities you participate in during Higher Still Physical Education your performance should aim to develop your repertoire (range) of skills and techniques, decision-making and control and fluency.

Swimming example

REPERTOIRE	DECISION-MAKING	CONTROL, FLUENCY
You should be competent in most of the key elements of two major strokes (frontcrawl, backcrawl or breaststroke). This should be shown in your body position, leg action, arm action, breathing and timing when swimming. Starts should be appropriate to stroke and with an effective flight, entry and glide phase. There should be little loss of momentum as the body completes turns in any of the three major strokes. You should be able to maintain your pace to the finish.	The performance of each stroke should be in demanding contexts where the key elements of each stroke are sustained during the swim. This should be reflected in the interval times taken. Swimming should be against performers of similar ability over distances of at least 50 m. This could involve intra or inter class, inter house or inter school galas or special events such as qualifying heats for club events.	You should show a high degree of control and fluency in each key aspect of the major strokes. In frontcrawl and backcrawl, for example, the body position should be streamlined with the leg action alternating and continuous, balancing the movements of the arms. Breathing should not affect the fluency of the stroke pattern and should be regular and controlled. The timing should be smooth, balanced and constant.

Your performance is assessed in two activities. Each activity is marked out of 20 marks. You need to gain 11 marks or more to achieve the Performance Unit. The two marks out of 20 you achieve are added together to arrive at your final Performance mark for the Course award. For example, if you scored 17 marks for one activity and 14 for the second activity, you would achieve a final Performance mark of 31 marks out of the 40 marks available.

Your performance work is **assessed on a continuous basis** throughout the session by your teacher(s). As your performance is judged continuously, work out an **improvement plan** for your level of performance.

Ensure that you know the two activities in your course that count towards your final Assessment. For example, if gymnastics, swimming and basketball are the three activities in your course, work out which two are most likely to be included in your final grade. Concentrate on these two outside your centre for performance improvement. If your ability is roughly equal across both activities, ensure you spend time developing each of them. Check your judgements with your teacher.

Check on your performance profile. If you are a very high-level performer in one activity, the development of your second activity may increase your mark on the performance scale when it comes to aggregating your marks.

Analysis and Development of Performance

Unit Assessment

The assessment instrument for this Unit is an assignment. The assignment provides a record of your work as you investigate and develop an aspect of your performance. The assignment process is structured to allow you to record each stage of your analysis, and to show how relevant Key Concept knowledge was understood and applied in the planning of a programme of work. Finally, an evaluation of the effectiveness of the analysis and development process is completed.

The assignment requires you to apply knowledge from a minimum of two Key Concepts from a specific area of analysis of performance. You should understand how the demands of the unit assignment link to the process of analysing performance and to specific Key Concepts. The greater detail you use to provide explanations about how you collected information and Key Concepts the better. This will help you to make detailed judgements when analysing performance, to explain how you monitored your performance when training and how you evaluated your chosen course of action.

To complete the assignment, you choose an aspect of your performance from the activities you are taking part in during your Physical Education course. The programme of work you complete should last for enough time for you to discuss and evaluate how your performance has progressed. You are required to complete **one assignment** from one area of analysis of performance.

Timing and duration of assessment

Your teacher will advise you on whether you will complete one assessment of up to one and a half hours or two shorter assessments of up to 45 minutes each. For example, your might complete the first two learning outcomes in your assignment in the first 45 minute assessment and the second two learning outcomes in the second assessment. Your teacher will ensure that you have completed sufficient work before you begin your assessment and will provide you with regular feedback about the standard of your assignment answer.

Completing the Unit assignment

To achieve a Unit you must pass each of the four Outcomes in one area of Analysis and Development of Performance. To achieve each Outcome you need to answer a number of questions which relate to your analysis. Try to produce the very best assignment you can. This will help your centre estimate how well you are likely to do in your Course Assessment. Try to ensure that your Unit answers are as full and detailed as possible. If necessary, you are normally allowed one opportunity to be reassessed.

When completing your Unit Assessment in the Analysis and Development of Performance Unit you are required to link your answer to two Key Concepts. Understanding which two Key Concepts you are focusing on is important. So, check that you are familiar with the Key Concepts in the different areas of analysis of performance. The table on page 35–36 contains all the Key Concepts in each area of Analysis and Development of Performance.

UNIT AND COURSE ASSESSMENT PROCESS

When completing the assignment you complete work in a number of different stages. These are:

- **Investigate** where you explain how a specific aspect of performance was investigated through gathering information
- **Analyse** where you explain in detail how knowledge from Key Concepts helped you to analyse performance
- **Develop** where you complete a programme of work and explain how the programme was monitored
- **Review / Evaluate** where you reflect on the effectiveness of the programme of work and discuss future performance needs.

The assignment stages match the different Outcomes and performance criteria for the Unit.

Intermediate 2

Stage	Outcomes	Performance Criteria
Investigate	1 Explain performance in an activity	(a) Methods selected and used for observing and recording data are valid (b) Data gathered are valid (c) Performance strengths and weaknesses are explained (d) Development needs are explained
Analyse	2 Use Knowledge and Understanding to analyse performance	(a) Relevant Key Concepts and key features are selected and used to analyse performance (b) Relevant information sources are used to plan performance development (c) A programme of work is designed to meet identified needs
Develop	3 Monitor a programme of work	(a) A relevant programme of work to meet identified needs is completed (b) The content of the programme of work is monitored (c) Performance development is monitored
Review	4 Review the analysis and development process	(a) The effectiveness of the analysis and development process is explained (b) The effects on performance are explained (c) Future development needs are explained

Stage	Outcomes	Performance Criteria
Investigate	1 Analyse performance in an activity	(a) Methods selected and used for observing and recording data are valid (b) Data gathered are valid (c) Performance strengths and weaknesses are valid (d) Development needs are analysed
Analyse	2 Use Knowledge and Understanding to analyse performance	(a) Relevant Key Concepts and key features are selected and used to analyse performance in detail (b) Relevant information sources are used effectively to plan performance development (c) A programme of work is designed to effectively address identified needs
Develop	3 Monitor a programme of work	(a) A relevant programme of work to address identified needs is completed (b) The content and demand of the programme of work is monitored (c) Performance development is monitored effectively
Evaluate	4 Evaluate the analysis and development process	(a) The effectiveness of the analysis and development process is discussed (b) The effects on performance are discussed (c) Future development needs are discussed

 At Higher level, you are required to move from explaining to discussing and from reviewing to evaluating. To help you, try to focus on the effectiveness of your performance improvement and on the processes you completed for analysing your performance.

COURSE ASSESSMENT, EXAMPLES OF QUESTIONS, WORDING OF QUESTIONS

Course Assessment

In your answers you must show the ability to:

Investigate performance and give clear, full and detailed explanations about your performance.

Analyse performance and show that you understand all relevant Key Concepts and can make sound judgements.

Develop performance by designing and monitoring a programme of work.

Evaluate and analyse performance improvements.

Ensure that your answer is based on the relevant Key Concepts. For example, if you are answering a *Performance Appreciation* question, make sure your answer relates to the Key Concepts in this area that the question is asking about.

Your answers will be marked by Physical Education teachers working for the Scottish Qualifications Authority (SQA). These markers will read your answers thoroughly and award marks based on the ability (competence) that you have shown. The main requirement is that your answers are as **full and detailed** as possible.

The demands of the Unit Assessment are very similar to those of the Course Assessment. Therefore, the better you do at the Unit Assessment, the greater the chance there is of you **transferring** your understanding from your Unit answers to your Course answers.

To produce examination answers that reflect your ability, it is useful to practise answering questions under examination conditions. This will help you to cope with the **time demands** of writing under examination conditions and will test your ability to **retain and recall** the fine detail of your course experiences and the understanding you developed from practical learning.

After you have completed the two Units that make up a Course award there should be time available for you to further practise developing your answers. Use this time productively, in the time before the Course examination.

Examples of Course questions

Here are four example questions, one from each area of Analysis of Performance. You should be able to see some **differences** and some **similarities** in the way the questions are set out.

---

1 Performance Appreciation (Higher)

From **one** activity in your course:

(a) Describe the **nature** and **demands** of the activity, as you worked towards improving the overall **quality** of your performance. **6**

(b) Explain the major **strengths** and **weaknesses** in the overall **quality** of your performance. **4**

(c) For the weaknesses identified in part (b) above explain the plan of action you followed to improve your quality of performance. **6**

(d) Evaluate the effectiveness of the plan of action you followed in terms of improving the quality of performance. **4**

(20)

---

2 Preparation of the Body (Intermediate 2)

Choose **one** activity from your course.

Physical aspects of fitness	Skill-related aspects of fitness	Mental aspects of fitness
cardiorespiratory endurance	reaction time	level of arousal
local muscular endurance	agility	nature of motivation
strength	co-ordination	mental rehearsal
speed	balance	managing stress
power	timing	
flexibility		

Continued on next page

(a)   Choose **two physical aspects of fitness** and explain their importance in developing your performance in the activity you have chosen.   **6**

(b)   Choose **one** aspect of either **skill-related OR mental aspect of fitness** and explain its importance in developing your performance in the activity you have chosen.   **4**

(c)   For one of the aspects of fitness you have chosen in parts (a) or (b) describe how you **collected information** on this aspect of fitness.   **4**

(d)   Explain briefly how you **planned** a training programme for the aspect of fitness you collected information on in part (c).   **3**

(e)   Explain briefly how you **evaluated** a training programme for the aspect of fitness you collected information on in part (d).   **3**

            (20)

---

3 Skills and Techniques (Higher)

Choose **one** activity.

When analysing your performance you will have used one of the following methods.

Mechanical analysis   Movement analysis
Consideration of quality

(a)   Choose one of the methods above. Explain in detail how this method was useful for collecting information about your performance.   **6**

(b)   Using the information collected in part (a), describe your Analysis of Performance's results.   **4**

(c)   Your performance will have been affected by:

     Motivation   Concentration   Feedback

     Explain the importance of **one** of the factors in the development of your performance.   **6**

(d)   Explain how you evaluated your performance with regard to the factor chosen in part (c).   **4**

            (20)

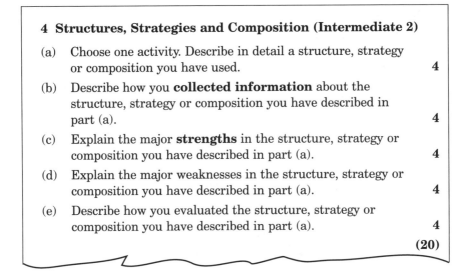

4 Structures, Strategies and Composition (Intermediate 2)

(a) Choose one activity. Describe in detail a structure, strategy or composition you have used. **4**

(b) Describe how you **collected information** about the structure, strategy or composition you have described in part (a). **4**

(c) Explain the major **strengths** in the structure, strategy or composition you have described in part (a). **4**

(d) Explain the major weaknesses in the structure, strategy or composition you have described in part (a). **4**

(e) Describe how you evaluated the structure, strategy or composition you have described in part (a). **4**

(20)

You should be able to see some **similarities** in each of these questions. They are all meant to be open and accessible. This means that they can be answered from whatever activities and experiences you have had on your course. You should also be able to see some slight **differences** in the way the questions are set out. The Intermediate 2 level questions tend to have more sections with a small number of marks for each section. The Higher level questions tend to have fewer sections but each section is worth more marks.

Types of questions

There tend to be two types of Course examination questions. There are those where the **process** is clearly apparent from the question's wording. Questions 1 and 4 above are examples of this type of question. In these questions you should be able to see how the different parts of the question link to the four stages involved in the Cycle of Analysis. Next, there are questions where the **content** of the question is much more prominent. Questions 2 and 3 above are examples of this type of question. In answering these questions ensure that the content of your answer links to relevant Analysis of Performance processes as often as possible.

Wording of questions

The wording of questions (as well as the marks available) will provide you with an insight into the level of detail required within your answer. Try to take account of the **active verbs** that are included within questions. The diagram below indicates how an increase in the demands of the active verb used will be reflected in the difficulty of the question and the marks available.

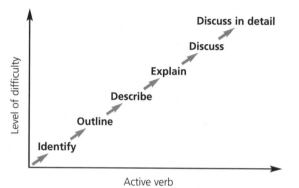

IMPROVING YOUR WRITING SKILLS

In your course aim to use appropriate and effective language during all parts of Higher Still PE; for example, when:

- speaking with other students and teachers about performance-related ideas
- using diagrams, graphs and statistics to explain performance
- completing assessment answers using correct grammar and presentation.

Speaking with other students and teachers about performance-related ideas

- All subjects at Intermediate 2 and Higher level contain their own specialised language.
- In PE, understanding words and terms relating to performance and the analysis and development of performance is vital.
- The Key Words Checklist on pages 125 to 126 highlights many of the most important (key) words which relate to the different Key Concepts.
- Practise using these words in their correct context when discussing performance-related ideas with students and teachers.

- Take time to clarify the exact meaning of the key words. It is important, for example, that your understanding of words like motivation, concentration and feedback is identical to other students and your teacher.

- Record in you planner definitions of key words and use this as a study aid when completing homework tasks.

Using diagrams, graphs and statistics to explain performance

Diagrams

- 'A picture paints a thousand words' is a common saying and one that is often true for Intermediate 2 and Higher level PE.

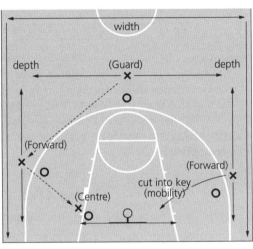

- A simple but clear diagram can explain relevant details quickly and accurately. For example, this diagram shows the importance of team principles (width, depth and mobility) within a 4 v 4 basketball game.

- You should practise drawing simple diagrams as part of your preparation for the Course examination in Analysis and Development of Performance.

- Diagrams should be clear and precise, and easy and time-saving to produce.

- All that is required are neat lines and simple lettering.

Graphs

- Graphs are another useful way of displaying useful information on performance.

- Graphs can be used to reference performance, for example, in terms of physical fitness levels.

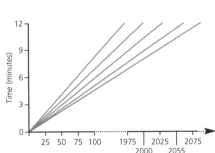

- Comparisons of aspects of performance can be displayed by a graph, for example, the physical fitness levels of different performers relative to fitness test norms.

Statistics

- Statistics are a useful way for describing performance. For example, in the comparison of two tennis players below, statistics show that Player A is better at returning serve than Player B.

Player A	Performance criterion	Player B
	Returns	
64%	All returns in	58%
66%	Forehand returns in	62%
62%	Backhand returns in	54%

- Statistics can also make explanations of performance simpler to comprehend. For example, it might be easier to describe how a player shooting in basketball was successful with just over of a third (35%) of shots, rather than stating that they scored with 7 out of 20 shots.

Completing assessment answers using correct grammar and presentation

Grammar – Tenses

- For the majority of your writing about analysis and development of performance you require to use the past tense.
- This is because you are reporting on the first three outcomes of the Cycle of Analysis, namely investigating, analysing and developing performance.

Check the difference between the past and present tense.

Tense	Writing style	
Past tense	When I completed the 800 m running race	✔
Present	I am completing the 800 m running race	✘

- It is only when you are completing the last stage of the Cycle of Analysis – reviewing and evaluating performance – that you sometimes use the future tense.
- Using the future tense would be useful when explaining your next performance goals.

Tense	Writing style	
Future	My target in future 800 m running races will be …	✔

Grammar – Linking phrases

- Clear, fluent writing is enhanced by carefully using different linking phrases.
- These are most commonly used at the beginning of sentences and are helpful in explaining what you did next and why it was important.
- Using short linking phrases helps avoid longer sentences, which can sometimes be difficult to understand.
- Linking phrases can explain what you did next, for example 'Consequently', 'Accordingly'.
- Linking phrases can be helpful when you are comparing and contrasting aspects of performance, for example 'On the other hand', 'Alternatively'.

Common linking phrases

In contrast	**At the same time**	**Moreover**	**On the other hand**
A case in point	**Next**	**Unlike**	**Alternatively**	**Consequently**
	Furthermore	**However**	**Accordingly**	

Presentation

The following points are designed to help make your writing clear, straightforward and easy to read and comprehend.

- The first key step is to ensure that your writing follows the chronological order of what you did and why it was important.
- Following this sequential writing frame will link your writing to the Cycle(s) of Analysis and to the outcomes of the Analysis and Development of Performance Unit.
- Signposting your explanation by very briefly introducing your answer is helpful, as is having a brief conclusion to each part of your answer.
- Always ensure you use paragraphs.

 Study the example of a good presentation below. Note the short introduction and conclusion. Note also how the use of 'firstly' and 'secondly' at the beginning of paragraphs helps explain the chronological order of what you did and why it was important.

(c) Describe, in detail, the methods of practice which you used to improve your ability in the chosen skill or technique with a view to improving your whole performance.

To refine my technique I used a series of progressive practices. This involved the use of repetition drills and pressure drills.

Firstly, I used repetition drills where I aimed at targets placed along the base of the serve box. This was in a 'closed' situation as I did not need to worry about the returned shot. This gave me a visual picture of the correct action and placement of my serve. I learned at this stage to reinforce my ball toss action, body positioning and follow through action. I also learned to adapt all of the aforementioned factors according to the type of serve selected. Depending on which target I was aiming at would reinforce my ability to place and vary the tempo and depth of my serve. Crucial to completing the serve effectively was an accurate ball toss. Feedback during these repetitive drills came mainly from myself – from the 'feel' of the action. If I missed the deep corner targets then I simply aimed to get the ball anywhere in the serve box for my second serve. This took the pressure off me. I repeated this several times making sure I aimed at each target 10 times. I monitored my success rate and rested before I repeated the drill from the left-hand side of the court. This was necessary to ensure I was effective on both sides.

Secondly, I progressed using pressure drills. These began by using the ball feed machine. Here, I could adjust the speed and direction of the return, which helped to develop my follow up attacking play. Next, I progressed to using partner pressure drills as I found this more challenging. Playing a person rather than a machine made the pressures more like the real thing. Basically, I found myself much more motivated to do well as I liked watching the response made by my partner as they worked to return my serve. The game-like nature developed my ability to make better decisions. The unpredictable responses made by my partner made me more alert and ready to respond with my follow up action. During these drills I was also able to develop other types of my fitness. I was also able to develop my mental fitness which is a very important aspect of the serve. I learned to control my emotions, fully concentrate on the task on hand and block out any unnecessary distractions. This also helped me not to panic when I 'double served'.

In conclusion, the closed then open nature of these practices helped me to improve my serving action. I was now much more confident of getting that very necessary first serve in.

9 Preparing For Your Analysis and Development of Performance Examination

Planning your answer

During the Course examination

PLANNING YOUR ANSWER

When planning a homework answer or completing an examination question it is useful to note down the key points you wish to include before beginning to write your answers.

> In your Analysis and Development of Performance Course examination spend the first 15 minutes reading all the questions and noting down the key points you wish to include. This still leaves you with 2 hours and 15 minutes to complete your three answers, an average of 45 minutes per question. This is ample time to write an excellent answer.

Develop the idea of a **'thought shower'**, where thinking and recording key points results in an answer plan, which links directly to the four learning outcomes – investigating, analysing, developing, and reviewing and evaluating performance.

Thought shower example 1

The following example of a thought shower is based on example 3: football and skills and techniques used earlier.

Outcome	What I did	Key points
Investigating	Observation schedule	• Compare performance against criteria • Evidence is valid and reliable and straightforward to comprehend • Useful for analysing a single technique (tackling) • Allows for repeated observation and follow up assessment
Analysing	Movement analysis	• The benefits of completing a movement analysis • Which area of my tackling required the greatest improvement – preparation, action or recovery? • How does my tackling compare with that of a model performer? • What were my areas of strength and weakness?
Developing	Plan of action	• Explaining the stage of skill learning of your tackling ability • Explaining the practice methods which were best for improving your tackling technique • Explaining relevant principles of effective practice • Explaining the importance of concentration when defending and tackling as a midfield player in football
Evaluating	Performance review	• Evaluate your ability at tackling in football in the context of competitive football games • Explain how your understanding of principles of effective practice methods in the context of football benefited performance

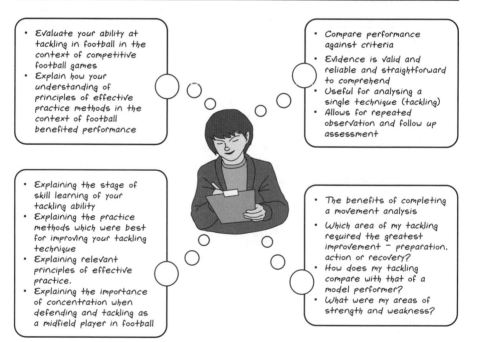

- Evaluate your ability at tackling in football in the context of competitive football games
- Explain how your understanding of principles of effective practice methods in the context of football benefited performance

- Compare performance against criteria
- Evidence is valid and reliable and straightforward to comprehend
- Useful for analysing a single technique (tackling)
- Allows for repeated observation and follow up assessment

- Explaining the stage of skill learning of your tackling ability
- Explaining the practice methods which were best for improving your tackling technique
- Explaining relevant principles of effective practice.
- Explaining the importance of concentration when defending and tackling as a midfield player in football

- The benefits of completing a movement analysis
- Which area of my tackling required the greatest improvement – preparation, action or recovery?
- How does my tackling compare with that of a model performer?
- What were my areas of strength and weakness?

Thought shower example 2

The following example of a thought shower is based on question 2 from the 2005 Specimen Question Paper. Check how the recording of the key points links directly to the answer provided.

Outcome	What I did	Key points
Investigating	Video Match analysis Specific questionnaire	• Video because accurate for measuring performance • Video suits activity which is fast paced and allows for repeated observation • Video enabled me to reference performance with match analysis and specific questionnaire sheets • Match analysis sheets measured my performance during each of the four quarters • Specific questionnaire sheets useful for evaluating my mental fitness
Analysing	Developing a training programme	• Specificity / conditioning through game related drills • Aimed to improve skill and mental aspects of fitness • Used 'self-talk' at beginning and end of training session • Practised drills under pressure, explain practice intervals • Explain work to rest intervals
Developing	Managing training over time	• How training programme was adapted and varied over time • Explain the progressions to practices which you used • Explain changes to structure of some practices
Evaluating	How training influenced performance	• Effects of controlling temper better • Benefits of control in being able to perform skills better • Improved anticipation benefits • Benefits from overall performance

2 Choose one activity.

(a) During your course you will have gathered data about different aspects of your whole performance in this activity. Discuss the significance of the information your data generated for two different aspects of your performance.

The data methods I used included the video, match analysis sheets and specific questionnaire sheet. I wanted to find out how effective I was in my role as a wing defence in netball. Specifically, I wanted to know if I performed my defending and attacking duties consistently throughout the game. I decided to use the video as this was the best tool of analysis to avoid human error. The game is fast paced and I did not want to miss anything. The video allowed me to look at my game several times which let me check my match analysis and questionnaire sheets to see if they backed up what I was seeing.

The match analysis was divided into five minute slots for each of the four quarters. I asked my marker to indicate the number of passes I made, the number of passes I tipped or intercepted, the number of times I forced my partner to commit a foul or time violation, the number of unforced errors I made. My questionnaire was designed specifically to evaluate my mental fitness. The specificity of the questions related to my success rate at controlling my temper; especially after making unforced errors or when the score was tight.

I was able to use these methods to define my strengths and weaknesses in my performance. The analysis of my data showed that I performed most of my defensive duties well. My percentages of interceptions, blocks and forced time violations were high; especially at the centre pass. I was not so consistent when performing my attacking duties, when our own GA and WA were being tightly marked. I should have been ready to get out and take this pass, instead I was slow to react to my centre requiring assistance and caused her to time violate. I was also mistiming my long feed into the circle and did not take enough notice of our opponents' GD; this meant I was throwing away potential shooting opportunities. I could see this first hand from the video action as I saw my poor ability to handle my emotions. This features as real weakness in my game and the results shown in my questionnaire reveal that on too many occasions I get caught up on poor umpire decisions, comments made by my opponents or indeed my dropped head and continual talking to myself when I make unforced errors.

(b)   Discuss how you have used this information to develop a training programme to meet your identified needs. For each aspect of your performance give specific examples of what you did.

I used this information to help me design a training programme that would effectively suit my needs. I knew to consider specificity and so used a conditioning approach to my training which included a series of repetition – and game-related – drills. This helped me to develop both my skill-related fitness and mental aspects of my performance at the same time. I also found this more motivating and suited me best. As the nature of the game relies on a team effort it was essential that I practised under similar game conditions. This helped me to produce a more consistent performance and helped me to adapt more quickly to the unexpected. I definitely needed to do something about my temper and it was suggested that I used 'self talk' to improve this. I was quite sceptical at this point! However the regime of deep breathing, focused thoughts and repeating in my head 'Keep calm – don't say anything – no facial expressions – walk away' forced me to reflect on my game performance. I did this 3–5 times before my training and again at the end of each session.

In role-related drills such as dodging / marking / throwing I made sure I worked under pressure; this improved my anticipation to cover space, reduce time and options for my opponent and heightened my awareness to move earlier to intercept. It also helped me to control my temper. For example, my coach told my WA to be quite aggressive and 'push me off the ball'. Instead of reacting back or 'giving up' I took a deep breath and remained focused; as a result I made greater effort to mark closer and press her.

The pressure drills of 'give and go' and 'box' practice were completed at various speeds. This again improved my anticipation and timing as I had to consider more than one cue at a time, for example, players were cutting into space sometimes 'open' sometimes 'marked', I was forced to consider options and make appropriate decisions. This was completed 3–5 times with a rest period in between.

I used repetition plays of set pieces such as centre passes, backline passes, side line throw-ins or penalty passes. This again forced me to practise my reaction time and anticipation in relation to the ball, the immediate situation and positioning of my team mates and the opposition. This helped sharpen my reaction speed, reinforced my passing accuracy and helped me to make better decisions. These plays were repeated 5 times first without opponents then with opponents to make it game like. I learned to respond to the 'unexpected' situations.

I made sure I varied the order of the drills, to make sure I did not get bored and took appropriate rests so that I did not get too tired.

> (c)   Describe how you managed your training over a period of time and explain any changes you made to your programme.

During my training period I knew to increase the intensity of my programme as I would have adapted to the previous one. I also did not want to become complacent as I feared I might slip back into old habits. I added different self talk statements so that I had a sequence of 3 different regimes I could use. This variation helped me to remain focused on controlling my temper. As well as doing this at the start and end of my training I would do it during rest periods as well; this helped me to reinforce new learned behaviour patterns. The more often I repeated these statements in my head the more calm and ready for action I seemed to become. The pressure drills were done more often and with more pressure added. For example, I would add in one more attacking player when doing my dodging / marking / throwing drill and did this 6–10 times – this helped me concentrate more.

I had learned that it was necessary to do more mass practice rather than distributed practice on occasions. I therefore changed the structure of the practice on occasions by ensuring a specific focus was made on one major area of weakness. For example, if our problem featured more on our centre pass play then I made sure we practised and concentrated solely on this for the biggest percentage of time. At other times I simply varied the drill order to avoid boredom or I would add increased pressure by adding in more players or simply increase the number of times the drill had to be completed.

The important factor about managing training over a period of time is the need to vary and adapt training to meet immediate requirements – I tried to do this.

(d)   Describe how your training influenced your ability to meet the demands of performance in your chosen activity.

The biggest impact my training had was on my ability to control my temper. I noticed (and so did my team) a big improvement in my ability to manage my emotions. I was less likely to talk back at my own players or the umpire which meant I remained focused on what I was supposed to be doing. When I made a mistake I simply made myself more determined to get the ball back. I looked more positively at things and realised that the best way to attack was to be a more controlled player. Even when the game was tight I found myself encouraging players to get the ball back. This in turn led to improved statistics in my ability to make better decisions; I remained focused and contributed very positively to the game.

Very importantly this helped me to apply my other skills more effectively. Being more in control meant that I more effectively fulfilled my role related duties. My pressure and problem solving drills had made my anticipation sharper; as a result I moved to assist my team mates more consistently and was causing my opposite number to make more mistakes. I also took a split second more to time my passes and so made fewer mistakes. My long feed passes directly into the shooting circle were more accurate as I was timing the pass well ahead of my GA and GS. I judged better the options available to me and made sure I used the safer short pass if the risky long ball was not on.

I consider myself a much more rounded player and know that I meet the demands of my role and the game much better than before.

DURING THE COURSE EXAMINATION

Once you have decided which three sections of the exam paper you will answer:

- Take time to read all the questions from each section and choose the one you find most straightforward to answer.
- Study how the marks are awarded in each question. For example, if the question parts are awarded as 4, 4, 8 and 4 marks, ensure that you are well aware of what is required in the 8-mark section of the question.
- Allocate the correct amount of time to each part of each question. Spend more time answering a section worth 8 marks than a section worth 4. Monitor your time closely.
- Plan an outline of your answer prior to beginning your answer. Avoid being rushed into starting before your thoughts are complete.
- Keep the context of your answer centered on your performance, either as an individual or as part of a group or team.
- Ensure your answers avoid repetition. Each part of the question is asking something specific. You do not have time for unnecessary detail or vague writing.
- Try to keep the thread of your answer going. Concentrate only on exactly what the question is asking.
- Allocate equal time to each section. You need to complete three good answers. Remember that one poorly answered or half-answered question will lower your overall mark.

10 Assessment Examples

Course Assessment: Performance Appreciation (Higher level)

Unit Assessment: Preparation of the Body (Intermediate 2 level)

Unit Assessment: Skills and Techniques (Higher level)

Course Assessment: Structures, Strategies and Composition (Intermediate 2 level)

Close scrutiny of these examples will provide helpful insights into what makes a very good answer.

The examples shown include:

- Course Assessment at Higher level (Performance Appreciation)
- Unit Assessment at Intermediate 2 level (Preparation of the Body)
- Unit Assessment at Higher level (Skills and Techniques)
- Course Assessment at Intermediate 2 level (Structures, Strategies and Composition)

COURSE ASSESSMENT: PERFORMANCE APPRECIATION (HIGHER LEVEL)

From **one** activity in your course:

(a) Describe the **nature** and **demands** of the activity, as you worked towards improving the overall **quality** of your performance.   **6**

(b) Explain the major **strengths** and **weaknesses** in the overall **quality** of your performance.   **4**

(c) For the weaknesses identified in part (b) above explain the plan of action you followed to improve your quality of performance.   **6**

(d) Evaluate the effectiveness of the plan of action you followed in terms of improving the quality of performance.   **4**

   (20)

Chosen activity: Rugby Union

(a) Describe the **nature** and **demands** of the activity, as you worked towards improving the overall **quality** of your performance.   **6**

Playing rugby has many different demands to consider. Many of the demands are similar for all players in the team but some are specific to individual players who play in particular positions.

The nature of rugby presents its own special challenges. Rugby is directly competitive and this means that players need to have personal and physical qualities in order to succeed. Personal qualities such as determination, courage and the ability to work as part of a team are required by all players. For example, tackling requires courage.

Teacher comment
Good introduction of the link between nature of activity and personal qualities – more development of this link was required.

Working as part of a team involves agreeing how the team is going to play to its strengths. Because rugby teams have 15 players, it would be chaotic if each player played for him or herself instead of for the team. As a result, it will be necessary for forwards and backs, the two major groups of players in a team, to agree how the game is going to be played. Playing will often involve the forwards winning possession of the ball, then passing it quickly to the backs. Playing as part of a team will also be important in determining the speed and tempo of the game. For example, it would help us to decide whether we play a fast, open, attacking game or a close, tight, defensive game. I play as a stand-off half (number 10) so my role is crucial in decisions about following a game plan.

The knowledge shown about the importance of working as a team is very good and shows that the student has an awareness of different roles and responsibilities.

Physical qualities are also needed but these will differ according to a player's position. In my role, I need to be quite quick and quite strong. Other players, mostly the forwards (numbers 1–8), need to be particularly strong. For the backs that line up outside me (numbers 11–15), it is useful if they are quick. The scrum half (number 9) and I are often referred to as the 'link' players in the team as we link the forwards and backs. As well as being quite quick and strong, we also all need to sometimes show a lightness of touch, for example when we or the forwards set the ball back in rucks and when the backs are passing.

Useful team description of physical qualities is set out. More development of some of the physical qualities required with further game examples would have been useful.

4 marks out of 6 awarded: Clear, full and occasionally detailed description of nature and demands of performance.

 For more marks, you should give more detailed descriptions of physical demands and qualities. Further consideration of special qualities such as courage, which is mentioned briefly, would have been useful.

> (b)   Explain the major **strengths** and **weaknesses** in the overall **quality** of your performance.   4

I have been playing rugby for many years. Overall, I consider that my performance has steadily improved. However, I think that some qualities within my performance are showing better progress than others. Physically, I have always been strong in the tackle and I have always taken responsibility for tackling when necessary even though I am a fair bit smaller than many other players.

Good introductory paragraph that sets context for later discussion on strengths and weaknesses.

My teachers and coaches have also been pleased with my commitment to the team and my intentions towards playing to the agreed team plan, whether this is based on either a fast, passing game or tighter, kicking game. As a result, my **personal** commitment to the team has never been in doubt. I have also managed to stay calm under pressure and this has been reflected in the way that I have encouraged my team-mates rather than criticised them during the game.

Some useful development of points made about personal qualities in part (a) of the answer.

My most noticeable weaknesses are in the **technical** and **special** qualities involved in my performance. When we are playing a fast, attacking game, the backs tend to line up in a 'flat line' which involves being close to the other team. This is a high-risk strategy. The idea is that by playing this way we can put pressure on the opposing players as early as possible to break over their gain line and maintain an attacking advantage. We prefer this to playing in a deeper line and often kicking the ball forward which would risk giving away possession at an early stage. My technical weakness when playing this way is that I can lack consistency when having to make moves quickly. I tend to rush and this can lead to losing possession through choosing poor options, such as trying to make a break when there is little space available or making a poor pass. I feel that developing some special performance qualities such as flair and deception would create uncertainty in the opposing team.

Very good linking of detailed knowledge about relevant technical and special qualities.

4 marks out of 4 awarded: Clear, full and detailed explanation that uses a full range of relevant concepts to make detailed judgements.

> (c)   For the weaknesses identified in part (b) above explain the plan of action you followed to improve your quality of performance.   **6**

The plan of action I followed was to undertake some problem-solving practices which revolved around making split-second decisions and adapting to what happens after decisions have been made. Clear objectives were set for these practices: these were set out and agreed by the teachers and the players. For example, we would set up practices where the aim was to get beyond the gain line as soon as possible. Other practices involved passing the ball along the line as quickly as possible. Some practices involved one of 'our' players deliberately running straight at 'opposing' players and trying to knock them over. This is called a 'crash ball'. If 'our' player is tackled, then we try to 'recycle' the ball as quick as possible and keep play moving forward.

Useful introduction about the practice plan of action that is intended is outlined.

The key point about all these practices is that they were meant to be as near to a full game as possible. The degree of difficulty in these practices was altered in various ways. For example, we altered how flat we played. The flatter our line was, the more difficult the practices were. Difficulty was also added by the 'opposing' players playing full opposition in the practices or reduced slightly by playing against a bit less than full opposition. The main idea behind the practices was that they had to have a quality focus. As a result, the time we spent on these practices was relatively short: usually about 15 minutes within an overall 75-minute training session.

The link between practices and game settings is well made. However, more detail on the progressions involved within the practices and how as a result the practices became increasingly demanding would have been useful.

These practices were very useful for me as they specifically addressed my technical weaknesses. I had to make decisions under time pressure and select options that I could consistently carry out well. It also gave me the opportunity to work out solutions that were unusual and that I had not tried before. As a result, I became more confident at trying out new moves for real during a game.

Some useful points about the relevance of the practices are made.

4 marks out of 6 awarded: A clear, full and occasionally detailed explanation about a course of action that is likely to lead to improvement is outlined.

> (d)   Evaluate the effectiveness of the plan of action you followed
>   in terms of improving the quality of performance.   **4**

The evaluation of the effectiveness of the training programme will only be possible after we have played a range of different types of rugby games which call for the implementation of different types of alignment amongst the back players. As a collective back unit, the training exercises appear to be useful because they have made us focus on taking what we have understood from our practices out onto the pitch.

A recognition of the need to reference practices against game performance is mentioned but regrettably not included with supporting game statistics, etc.

To make more definite judgements, it will also be useful to consider in future game analyses how well we played after longer phases of action. This would mean that, for example, even if we played a 'crash ball' strategy the initial first phase move might not get us to much progress. However, we might be able to recycle the ball and make effective progress in the second phase of our attack.

Some relevant areas of game performance for evaluation are indicated.

2 marks out of 4 awarded: Some clear and satisfactory suggestions for improvement are outlined.

Total: 14 out of 20 marks awarded

UNIT ASSESSMENT: PREPARATION OF THE BODY (INTERMEDIATE 2 LEVEL)

Your Unit assignment takes you through different analysis stages. You begin your assignment by selecting the activity, area of Analysis and Development of Performance and specific aspect of performance you will be trying to improve.

Activity: Hockey
Area of Analysis and Development of Performance: Preparation of the Body
Specific aspect of performance analysed: Skill-related fitness (agility) when dribbling in hockey

You then briefly explain the significance of this aspect to your whole performance.

> The main effect of my poor agility is that I get caught in possession and then the other team has the opportunity to get the ball. When dribbling, I can usually keep the stick close to the ball and as a result the ball is usually under control. This would indicate that my skill was quite good. It is just that the other players chasing me had caught me up. This was due to my poor agility – the ability to move my body quickly and precisely.

You then need to begin the **Investigation** process through collecting information about your performance. In this example, game analysis sheets have been used for both the initial and focused levels of data collection.

Initial level of data collection

> I had the following game analysis sheet completed. This allowed me to find out about my speed in a seven-a-side hockey game lasting 30 minutes each half.

Game Analysis Sheet

Team: Scotstown Academy   **Role:** Attacker
Opposition: Central High School   **Date:** 00/00/00

Type of speed measured	Role in game	1st half	2nd half
Getting free in attack (Short sprint)	Attacking	✔✔✔✔✔✔	✔✔✔
Getting free in attack (Long sprint)	Attacking	✔✔✔	✔✔✔
Dribbling (Short sprint)	Attacking	✔✔✔	✔
Dribbling (Long sprint)	Attacking	✔✔✔✔✔	
Getting back in defence (Short sprint)	Attacking	✔✔✔✔	✔✔✔✔
Getting back in defence (Long sprint)	Attacking	✔✔✔✔	✔✔✔
	✔ = effective		

Personal review: From this data I found out roughly how fit I was for sprinting in a seven-a-side hockey game. As a forward, I try to get free by losing my marker and by dribbling the ball forward into space. When defending, I also need to get back to help my team in midfield. The results show that I can mostly keep sprinting pretty well throughout the game but my dribbling gets less useful as the game goes on.

Focused level of data collection

I had the following game analysis sheet completed. This allowed me to find out about my sprinting when dribbling in a seven-a-side hockey game lasting 30 minutes each half.

Game Analysis Sheet

Team: Scotstown Academy   **Role:** Attacker
Opposition: Central High School   **Date:** 00/00/00

Type of speed measured	Role in game	1st half	2nd half
Dribbling unopposed (Short sprint)	Attacking in space	✔✔	✔✔ X X
Dribbling unopposed (Long sprint)	Attacking in space	✔ X	✔ X X
Dribbling opposed (Short sprint)	Attacking under pressure	✔✔ X	✔ X X
Dribbling opposed (Long sprint)	Attacking under pressure	✔✔ X	X X X
Reverse stick dribble	Wide in attack	✔ X	X X
	✔ = effective X = ineffective		

Personal review: I looked at my dribbling speed in more detail. I looked at how often in a game I was able to sprint and dribble well and how often I was ineffective in doing this.

Once you have collected this data, you can then go on to answer the Unit Outcome questions.

> Remember: With your Unit Assessments you are able to directly use the data that you have collected in the answering of your question. The answers to Outcomes 1–4 are based on the data collected on the game analysis sheets above.

Outcome 1: Explain performance in an activity

PC (a)   Methods selected and used for observing and recording data are valid

PC (b)   Data gathered are valid

PC (c)   Performance strengths and weaknesses are explained

PC (d)   Development needs are explained

Outcome questions

Student example answer

Explain the main information you collected from the data.

I think the way I collected information worked well. It was important that I collected information about what I was doing in a full game, rather than in my practices. The first game analysis sheet allowed me to look at my sprint speed both when I was just sprinting and also when I was trying to sprint and dribble the ball at the same time. The second sheet allowed me to consider my dribbling in more detail. This was good as dribbling was the part of the game I was poorest at doing.

Teacher example comment
The importance of using whole performance (games) for collecting information is well made as is the transfer between initial (general) and focused (specific) data.

Explain why the methods you used to record data were valid.

> The layout of the sheets was helpful. The sheets were well set out and easy to fill in, even during a fast game. This is because they were clear and well set out with plenty of space within the boxes. They also allowed me to add my own comments on how well I thought I had done. This will be helpful for me to look back on later.

Relevant points about how the observation sheets are to be completed are outlined.

Explain how your data helped you recognise your performance strengths and weaknesses.

> The data has shown me a lot of useful things about my level of fitness in hockey. Basically, I found out more and more detailed information as I went on. To start with, from my initial data I found that I had two problems.
>
> The first one was that I seemed to make fewer sprints as the game went on. You can see this from the reduced number of ticks for the second half as compared to the first half. The second problem I found was that I was less effective at dribbling quickly with the ball than I was at straight sprinting. Being able to dribble quickly is important in my position.
>
> The results of my data were quite useful for me. This is good because it told me accurately what I needed to work on. My problems seemed to be that I got tired as the game went on. This could let my performance down. More importantly, it showed that my agility when dribbling in hockey was not very good.

The correct identification of two relevant performance issues has been explained.

Explain how your data helped you recognise your development needs.

> The main thing that I needed to work on was my agility. I could sprint quite well, better in the first half than second half, but when dribbling the ball and running in a different shape and changing direction a lot, I found it difficult to keep my speed up. I also seemed to be slow at turning: this was shown by my focused level data. My mistake rate was quite high. I needed to work on agility.

The usefulness of the initial data in highlighting a specific performance issue has been quite carefully explained.

I tended to slow up too much to turn quickly. I think that sometimes I was driving off the wrong foot and this affected my balance when moving. For example, when dribbling forward with the ball on my left hand side, I would often try to knock the ball back over to my right hand side on the move. Often I would be doing this when my left foot (instead of my right foot) was forward. This was complicated and awkward. Being able to change direction is important for forwards because it allows them to get free of and go past defenders, either with or without the ball.

Further clarity about the importance of agility to forward play in hockey is outlined.

The midfield players in my team rely on me, one of the forwards, to make attacking breaks and to keep possession of the ball when I'm trying to get deep into the attacking half of the pitch. To do this, I needed to work on my agility. Better agility meant less risk of getting caught in possession and remaining in control of the ball as I would be able to move quicker and stay in better balance. If I could keep my agility at a good rate throughout the game this would help as well.

Relevant link to skill-related aspect of fitness and its importance within a game of hockey is made. Some further game-related examples of how this affected game performance would have been useful.

Outcome 2: Use Knowledge and Understanding to Analyse Performance

PC (a)   Relevant Key Concepts and key features are selected and used to analyse performance

PC (b)   Relevant information sources are used to plan performance development

PC (c)   A programme of work is designed to meet identified needs

To complete this next stage of the assignment you need to link your data to relevant Key Concepts. This will help you to analyse your performance and plan a development programme. Each assignment answer requires to link to two Key Concepts. You might find it useful to specify the key features you are using to help your analysis as well.

Key Concept 1	Application of different types of fitness in the development of activity specific performance
Key feature	Examine the performance requirement and related fitness needs for selected activities
Key Concept 2	Principles and methods of training.
Key feature	Select an appropriate method of training to develop one or more aspect of fitness (in this example, agility).

Key Concept 1

Explain the information about your performance you obtained from the study of this Key Concept.

> The main points I learned about in this key concept was that if you want to improve skill-related fitness then you need to train in specific skill-related performance contexts. Specificity is the most important part of a training programme so you need to make sure your training is specific. For example, in hockey I need to ensure that any conditioned games or practices are organised to ensure that they develop my agility. I know that practice must be specific to be useful and once you have achieved this you can then make the practice more demanding as time goes on. This is called adding overload to your training. In my case this would involve completing the practices quicker and possibly for longer as this is what I need to do to become a better player.

Information about the training principle of specificity is useful. The reference to how specificity links to performance in hockey is quite well made.

Discuss how you applied this information when designing a relevant development programme.

> I worked on my agility with a series of maze-type runs. I performed these as sets of sprints as well as occasionally performing them with hockey dribbles. I set up my training on a circuit of exercises of different levels of difficulty. The idea of the maze runs and the hockey dribbles was that they matched the demands of dribbling in a game. Therefore, they could be considered to be specific to my needs. We moved around the circuit twice. This was good as it seemed that we got the benefit of the practice, but not too much of the same thing that we got bored. It meant as well that my heart rate was always quite high. This would also help me on the endurance side of things as well.

Training is relevant to skill-related fitness as is mention of training for a suitable amount of time.

Key Concept 2

Explain the information about your performance you obtained from the study of this Key Concept.

Knowing that I had to make my training specific, I then went on to learn that there were two different ways to achieve this. I could either complete training on its own outside of the activity or by conditioning, which involved training through practices which link to the activity. I found out that both forms of training can be effective and that it depends on what your needs are which method of training you select. My practices were a conditioning approach, as I was actually dribbling the ball some of the time as well as trying to run quicker and more often. If I was only sprinting, for example, then this would have been training outside of the activity. However, the agility practice I was completing had a skill part to it as well as I was dribbling the ball. This helped make the training more realistic.

A grasp of the two most common types of practice is evident. This helps show evidence of the need to make any practice meaningful and realistic.

Discuss how you applied this information when designing a relevant development programme.

I made up a six item circuit with two of the exercises being about agility. One was a diagonal maze run like sprint and the other was the same type of sprint over the same distance but dribbling the hockey ball at the same time. The practices were 1 and 4 in the circuit to allow me to link these practices with other types of quite demanding fitness exercises in hockey.

The layout of the cones meant that I often had to change direction quickly and keep close control over the ball when moving at speed. The maze run involved a short 12 m sprint. I made sure that I mixed up the agility exercises within a larger fitness circuit so that I was not always practising the same type of thing and always using the same type of muscles. If I had done this I would have become tired more quickly. With tasks involving different muscle groups you were able to have some rest intervals in your training and keep practising for longer. This was good as it meant that I trained for about the same time as a game of hockey lasted.

Some evidence of specific practices is described. The idea of where to place practices in a circuit which have the same type of demand is well made.

Explain the training method you used and explain why you consider it was appropriate.

I think that this training method was useful as it was very specific to my exact agility needs. I think that if I had tried to achieve the same amount of practice benefit by either just running or playing games then this would not have happened. It was better to try and specifically practise on my weaknesses, but in a way that is realistic to my position in hockey and to my performance when I'm playing games of hockey.

I think circuit training was a useful practice method as the multi-stage circuit could include a good balance of some exercises which related to hockey in general and some specific exercises for agility.

Some further information about specificity has added to the depth of explanation. More detail on the merits of using circuit training would have been useful.

Explain the programme of work you designed to develop the selected aspect of performance.

After a warm-up, I performed a series of maze-type runs – these were 12 m each way. The cones were about 1m out to each side. This meant that I would need to move 2m across when going forward, cutting across from side to side. I had to make sure I pushed off my outside foot to stay in balance when moving. This would help save time as well as keeping me in a better balanced position when running. I would go once up and round, then back and rest. This would take about 8 seconds on average for the running only exercise. Then I would rest for 12 seconds and then go to the next station. The exercise in the circuit where I dribbled the hockey ball as well took a lot more time and varied more depending upon whether the ball went out to the side or not, or whether I lost control of it when at the top when turning. We moved between exercises every 30 secs and moved on at 20 secs. Mostly, this was when I was just arriving back at the start position.

Some useful detail about the practices that made up the plan of action is described.

Outcome 3: Monitor a Suitable Programme of Work

PC (a)   A relevant programme of work to meet identified needs is completed

PC (b)   The content of the programme of work is monitored

PC (c)   Performance development is monitored

To complete the next stage of the assignment you complete a programme of work. You explain how it was useful and how you monitored progress. Your programme should be long enough and demanding enough for you to gain the information necessary to discuss your performance.

Using a short table to keep a record of training diary / log of your completed training can be useful. See the example below.

Session	Brief reflections / evaluations on or about training
1	Week 2 – Monday. A good session. Gentle warm up appeared to help. The agility exercises were I thought quite demanding, especially the second time through the circuit.
2	Week 3 – Wednesday. I think that now is the time to add some more demand to the circuit. I think this because I feel that I am not working as hard as I was before. At the end tonight, I did not have to rest up for a few minutes before getting changed as I have done in previous training sessions.
3	Week 4 – The extra agility dribble that I have included has worked well. It makes the amount of specific exercise I do that bit more, but all in all I think this is a good idea for my training.

Explain how and why some parts of the programme were adapted as the programme progressed, or why you left the programme unchanged.

The main part of the programme remained unchanged for the first few weeks with my 2 repetitions of 6 exercises, built into my overall training session at which we also took part in practice games. After week 3 though I swapped the long hit and jog exercise in my circuit and replaced it with another agility hockey dribble. I switched the circuit around so that I did the agility run and hockey dribble as exercise number 1, 3 and 5 to keep them apart from the other exercises. I thought that this would be better as it would keep me practising the area of performance I most need to practise and I thought as the weeks went on that I could cope with the extra demand. The times I took for the running exercise show that this was the case.

Useful suggestions for adding to the specificity of training through adapting circuit.

Explain how you monitored the effect of your training programme.

I used time as the main way of working out whether my training was effective or not. For the single agility run my running speed was about 8 seconds and my rest was 12 seconds. I had a partner time my run to make sure that I kept up with this running time and that I did not get any slower.

I used time as well for the hockey dribble but this worked less well. This is because the time taken was less accurate. This is because sometimes you would lose control of the ball and this could add a lot of time to the time taken. I sorted this by trying to work out my average time from the 2 repetitions of the circuit. My target time was 20 seconds. Doing this was a help as it reduced the effect of having one poor exercise in the circuit.

Knowledge of results through monitoring time taken for exercises was useful evaluating training exercise effectiveness.

Outcome 4: Review the Analysis and Development Process

PC (a) The effectiveness of the analysis and development process is explained

PC (b) The effects on performance are explained

PC (c) Future development needs are described

To complete the final stage of your assignment you need to reflect on the effectiveness of the programme and explain any future development needs.

Explain the effect that the analysis and development process had on the selected aspect of performance.

My teacher always says 'There's only one way. We'll know whether your training programme worked when we get back to the game.' So this is what happened. The idea was to play more games after my weeks of working on my agility and see if I was a bit quicker.

The results showed that I had improved. I was better at getting away with the ball from other players. However, this was against generally poorer teams so this might have affected things. I still felt that I was moving a lot better and, crucially, that I was able to keep my balance a bit better when moving at top speed and not look awkward. This helped me keep better control of the ball. The next task is to check on my hockey dribbling and running when playing against better teams and whether I can keep this going all the way through the game, as I also need to work on this as well.

The link to skill-related fitness is continued and this adds to the relevance of the analysis completed.

Explain the effect that the analysis and development process had on your overall performance.

I think that having more control over the ball when dribbling has helped my overall performance. Being able to move a bit quicker away from defenders has allowed me to choose easier passing options. For example, if I can get past the defender and into space then you have a clearer passing channel whereas if the defender is close to you and you cannot dribble quickly away from them this makes your overall performance more difficult.

Useful linking of the benefits of training to increased effectiveness within role in hockey team.

Discuss your future development needs in this area of performance.

Now that my control and agility has improved as well as my ability to keep going all through the game, I think there is still a need to keep working on my basic running speed. I'm not the quickest and I think that if I can keep doing some sprint training then at least it will help me make the best of what I have got. So, this is what I think I need to do in the future. I need to work on a physical aspect of speed now that my skill-related aspect of fitness (agility) has got better.

Some reference and link to other aspects of fitness.

When explaining the effects on performance, remind yourself of what the 'Performance Outcome' in Higher Still Physical Education mentions. It looks at 'demonstrate effective performance in challenging contexts'. It mentions, in particular, the importance of 'a broad performance repertoire', 'appropriate decisions' and 'control and fluency'. Try to link your answer to these criteria when answering Outcome 4 on 'Review the analysis and development process'.

Unit Summary: This is a mostly coherent Unit answer which is at the Unit pass standard. There is some evidence of work above the minimum standard. The thread of the answer is quite well retained, as is the link between training and performance.

UNIT ASSESSMENT: SKILLS AND TECHNIQUES (HIGHER LEVEL)

Your Unit assignment takes you through different analysis stages. You begin your assignment by selecting the activity, area of Analysis and Development of Performance and specific aspect of performance you will be trying to improve.

Activity: Hockey
Area of Analysis and Development of Performance: Skills and Techniques
Specific aspect of performance analysed: Passing improvement through opposed / unopposed practices and conditioned, small-sided / coached games.

You then briefly explain the significance of this aspect to your whole performance.

> As an attacker, I have noticed from past games that my passing appears to be weak at times. This limits the effectiveness of my performance and the performance of my team. This is mostly because poor passing can limit our team's attacking options. Passing in attack, even over short distances, is always likely to be difficult as the defenders are likely to be working to their maximum to try and defend at this point.

You then need to begin the **Investigation** process through collecting information about your performance. There are a number of methods of information which might be useful for you to consider. Refer to these when choosing the best method for your investigation.

In this example, game analysis sheets have been used for both the initial and focused levels of data collection.

Initial level of data collection

> I had the following game analysis sheet completed. This allowed me to find out about my speed in a seven-a-side hockey game lasting 30 minutes each half.

Game Analysis Sheet

Team: *Scotstown Academy*   **Role:** *Attacker*
Opposition: *Central High School* **Date:** *00/00/00*

Time (minutes)	Control (first touch)	Passing (under 10 m)	Passing (over 10 m)	Dribbling	Tackling	Shooting
1st half 0–10	✔✔	✔		✔	✔	
11–19	✔✔	✔✔✔	✔✔	✔	✔✔	✔
21–30	✔	✔✔	✔	✔✔	✔	✔
2nd half 0–10	✔✔✔	✔✔ X X			✔	✔
11–19	✔✔	✔✔ X X	✔✔			✔
21–30	✔✔✔✔	✔✔✔ X	✔	✔		
✔ = effective X = ineffective						

Personal review: I analysed these results after the game. This allowed me to obtain feedback about my performance. I could see that for most of the game I contributed to our attack by performing my skills quite consistently. However, it appeared that my short passing was the poorest part of my game. This was as I expected it to be. It limited our attacking options. I felt very comfortable and had no problems lasting the 60 minutes. I decided to focus specifically on my short passing to see if I could find out more information.

Focused level of data collection

I had the following game analysis sheet completed. This allowed me to find out about my sprinting when dribbling in a seven-a-side hockey game lasting 30 minutes each half.

Game Analysis Sheet

Team: *Scotstown Academy*   Role: *Attacker*
Opposition: *Central High School*   Date: *00/00/00*

Time (minutes)	Pass forward under pressure	Pass forward under less pressure	Pass to side or back under pressure	Pass to side or back under little pressure
1st half 0–10	✔✔✔XX	✔	✔	✔✔
11–19	✔XX	✔✔	✔✔	✔
21–30	✔✔	✔✔	✔✔	✔
2nd half 0–10	✔		✔	✔✔✔
11–19	✔XX	✔✔	✔	✔✔
21–30	✔✔✔	✔✔	✔✔✔	✔
✔ = effective X = ineffective				

Personal review: The quantifiable evidence obtained from my movement analysis data confirmed my initial feelings that my occasionally unsatisfactory performance was due to poor passing under pressure. I was working hard as part of my team and I made lots of runs but, when under pressure, my passing was going astray. Most of my poor passes were overhit.

> **Remember:** With your Unit assessments you are able to directly use the data that you have collected in the answering of your question. The answers to Outcomes 1–4 are based on the data collected on the game analysis sheets above.

Outcome 1: Analyse Performance in an Activity

PC (a)　Methods selected and used for observing and recording data are valid

PC (b)　Data gathered are valid

PC (c)　Performance strengths and weaknesses are analysed

PC (d)　Development needs are analysed

Outcome questions

Student example answer

Explain the main information you collected from the data.

The initial data confirmed that it was my passing that was the most limited part of my game. It highlighted that my passing effectiveness was only at 50% for my short passing of less than 10 metres. Even though the pitch was quite small and that as an attacker I was closely marked this is still a low success rate. I made 16 passes during the 30 minute game and only half of the passes were effective. Other areas of my game like control were better. The initial data indicated that I controlled the ball with a good first touch on 11 out of 14 occasions. This indicates that getting the ball under control when 'on the deck' was not so much of a problem.

The focused data indicates that the major weakness was my passing under pressure. When defenders were close to me I tended to sometimes overhit passes almost as if I was panicking a little. The rest of my game was better and my effort as part of the team was well commented upon. What I needed though was a greater degree of accuracy in the timing and weight of pass when my team was attacking in the crucial last third of the pitch.

Teacher example comment

A useful outline explanation is provided which draws upon information collected from both the initial and focused data.

Explain why the methods you used to record data were valid.

I wanted the data to highlight how effectively I played in my role as a striker. The initial data showed what I suspected, namely that it was my passing that let me down the most. My other main striking skills were better. The initial data was appropriate because it looked at my whole game. The other thing that was good about it is that information was collected about both my first half and my second half performances. It was also clearly set out and easy to use. When I was observed carrying out certain skills by my class mates, my performances could be noted down.

To allow further depth of analysis, I used a detailed analysis sheet to collect my focused data. This data highlighted my effectiveness at passing both under pressure from defenders and when under less pressure. The method was reliable and easy to use, and allowed me to plan my later training programme. The criteria were also specific to the problem I had identified.

The development of data that was specific to passing under pressure was useful and appropriate for Higher level work.

Analyse how your data helped you recognise your performance strengths and weaknesses.

The results showed that my performance broke down slightly when I was under pressure. Passing is tricky under pressure. Players need to think about timing, weight and accuracy of pass. These are the most important things. My results showed that my timing, weight and accuracy broke down a bit when I was under pressure. I made only 6 effective penetrative forward passes when under pressure but 11 ineffective ones.

The data showed that I rarely made mistakes when under little pressure. My impression was that I overhit my passes when I was under pressure. I think I rushed things a bit and felt that if I give the ball a good hit then the pass would at least 'get there.' However, my other attackers often could not control the pass and the ball went on past them. Often they gave me a 'cold' look as well. This let me know that I'd hit the ball too hard again. My teacher said that it was good that I could recognise this look from my team mates. Feedback is very important in skill learning. However, possession is important in hockey and with the other teams being able to counter attack so quickly playing better passes was required.

Relevant knowledge about passing is apparent (timing, weight, accuracy) as is the link between this content knowledge and the student's own performance in a game of hockey.

Analyse how your data helped you recognise your development needs.

The data was very useful as it was specific to my performance. The data was relevant to the position I play in hockey and it was obtained against players of my own level of ability. Because of this accurate record of how I performed, I now feel that I am better prepared to design a relevant training programme, which is based on the exact parts of my overall game which require the most immediate attention. Moving from initial to focused data was useful as it helped move from something which I thought as a hunch was a problem to more detailed focus level data which highlight the specifics of the main part of my game which would benefit from improvement.

Clear link established between accurate data and development needs.

Outcome 2: Use Knowledge and Understanding to Analyse Performance

PC (a)   Relevant Key Concepts and key features are selected and used to analyse performance in detail

PC (b)   Relevant information sources are used effectively to plan performance development

PC (c)   A programme of work is designed to effectively address identified needs

To complete this next stage of the assignment you need to link your data to relevant Key Concepts. This will help you to analyse your performance and plan a development programme. Each assignment answer requires to link to two Key Concepts. You might find it useful to specify the key features you are using to help your analysis as well.

Key Concept 1	The concepts of skill and skilled performance
Key feature	How skills and techniques are performed for effective consistent performance while also displaying qualities of control, fluency and economy of movement
Key Concept 2	The development of skill and refinement of technique
Key feature	Methods of practice – opposed / unopposed and conditioned / small-sided and coached games

Outcome questions

Key Concept 1

Explain the information about your performance you obtained from the study of this Key Concept.

> As my weakness was overhitting passes, I needed to look at ways of playing short, accurate passes, which were hit just right when I was under pressure. What my passing required in order to be more effective was to make more controlled fluent passes where the right degree of effort was used, but which were played when I was in a tight situation where I was being marked. In a basic sense my passing was accurate but when passing under pressure the skill of passing is more complex and my performance level went down.

> The information from the data tended to suggest that when I saw the passing chance open up that I tended to hit the ball hard with the thinking being that this was the best way to get the ball through the gap. However, a hockey ball is both hard to stop and control for my team-mates and it is also quite difficult to intercept at times. Therefore, it would be much better and more skilled and effective if I played the ball with the correct weighting and timing. In doing this I gave my team mates a pass they could possibly continue the attack with. It would also add to my performance, if I could pass with the correct degree of effort and accuracy, as part of being a skilled hockey player is good stickwork with the necessary backlift and follow through. At present, I am taking too big a backswing and follow through than is necessary for a short pass.

Information about the concept of skilled performance in hockey is evident through reference to how control, fluency and economy of movement are required in hockey passing.

Discuss, in detail, how you applied this information when designing a relevant development programme.

> The first thing I had to do was organise game-related practices that would be specifically useful to me.

> I made sure that my skills training programme was effective. To do this, I took into account my specific needs. These were
> - playing passes quickly
> - playing passes at the right time

- using the correct weight in passing
- being accurate in my passing
- using economic movements (no excessive backlift or follow through)

Therefore, my knowledge of skilled performance was helpful in that it showed me that if you want to be better at short passing in a game then your training needs to involve some degree of active opposition. This reflects the fact that I needed to practise my passing by treating it as a complex skill and not a basic skill where there were no defenders involved.

I also required to consider my passing in attack in hockey as an open skill as it takes place during competitive play when there is direct competitive play and where you cannot be in control of the situation. For example, the defenders can move in unpredictable ways, which means that you also require to pay close attention to a range of different factors and adapt to what is happening in active situations.

Relevant knowledge about effective passing as part of skilled performance is evident. References to passing in hockey as open and complex skill are helpful for showing grasp of important factors which would influence design of training programme.

Key Concept 2

Explain the information about your performance you obtained from the study of this Key Concept.

On my course we have looked at a number of methods of practice. The key consideration is to make sure that you match the correct practice with the different skills and techniques you are trying to improve. Getting this connection correct is critical for making practice useful. One of the things which we learned about early on in our course is that inappropriate practice is futile.

What I was attempting to do with my passing was consolidate and make better a skill which I already knew about and could complete. What was required was the refinement of the skill rather than learning it from the beginning. This affects the method of practice that I choose. I needed a practice which was demanding and matched the demands of hockey games. From the range of practice methods that we have worked on during our course the best ones to use were opposed / unopposed and conditioned / small-sided game practices.

A grasp of two relevant forms of practice and how they link to the performance demands associated with hockey is evident.

Discuss, in detail, how you applied this information when designing a relevant development programme.

I next considered the specific practices I would work on and how I could make these more demanding as time went on. To avoid boredom and keeping my passing standard at the same level, I had to make sure that my practices replicated the demands of a game. This meant that after a warm up that we would spend say 20 minutes on opposed practices in boxes and small-sided conditioned games, before ending with a more competitive game.

The specific development of the opposed practices and conditioned games is quite carefully explained with suitable attention to detail.

The other thing I worked out was how long I would work for within the box practices. A few short practices are better than a session which is too long and so you might become bored and tired. I would work for a small burst of, say, 3 minutes, then rest, recover and practise again.

The opposed practices I worked on were completed in 10 m boxes. In these boxes, I used opponents to make me feel under pressure. I also made some of the practices more demanding by making sure that I had to take a first touch and then play the pass immediately. By adding difficulty like this, I was increasing the intensity of the practices. Taking a few touches and then turning around and looking are easier than playing the ball after one touch. The good think about small box work in hockey is that you can very easily add or take away the level of opposition. It is very important that the practice is challenging and achievable, but yet realistic and possible to do.

I also combined these practices with other skill practices so that my whole set of practices covered all areas of the game but, in my case, had a particular emphasis on passing under pressure. The other feature of my training was that during this time I was also involved in playing small-sided games and conditioned games. We spent about 10 minutes of the 20 minutes training having conditioned and small-sided games.

The emphasis on box passing practices within a larger hockey training programme is a valid point well made.

Analyse the training method you used and explain why you consider it was appropriate.

I think the main benefit of the training methods adopted was that active opposition was involved in both methods of practice. In the box practices with active opposition the 'rules' of the practice was that if the defenders gained possession of the ball then they switched and became attackers. This helped make the practice realistic for them. If it was the case that they had to defend for a few minutes then swap it is easy to predict that they would switch off from the practice and just move around and wait till they got their turn as attackers. For skills which are open and complex opposition is very useful. If it was possible to show control and fluency when practising then the practice transfer to full games would likely be higher.

The other addition of having this type of box practice and small-sided games was that the practice of skills was continuous as the practice and game just kept going for quite a few minutes. This was good as it kept everyone on task and also reflected the type of game which hockey is where play is continuous and everyone knows what to do at short corners and at free hits.

The reference to 'open', 'complex' and 'continuous' indicates that there is a clear understanding of effective practice linking with effective performance.

Analyse the programme of work you designed to develop the selected aspect of performance.

Overall, I do think that the practices adopted were effective as they clearly linked to my specific skill needs and my current ability level. The key consideration was to ensure that the practice was quality practice with the right degree of demand and that the amount of time spent on practice went on for a relatively short but suitable amount of time.

The reason why practice was short was that it was quite high in intensity. When in the boxes and games you had to be 'switched on' to all that was happening as there could be sudden changes as some passes went astray and as some interceptions were made. A high level of attention is required in open and complex practice settings.

The reasons provided to support the design of the training programme are quite well explained.

Outcome 3: Monitor a Programme of Work

PC (a)   A relevant programme of work to address identified needs is completed

PC (b)   The content and demand of the programme of work is monitored

PC (c)   Performance development is monitored effectively

To complete the next stage of the assignment you complete a programme of work. You explain how it was useful and how you monitored progress. Your programme should be long enough and demanding enough for you to gain the information necessary to discuss your performance.

Using a short table to keep a record of training diary / log of your completed training can be useful. See the example below.

Session	Brief reflections / evaluations on or about training
1	Week 1 – Monday. Good warm up, pitch in good condition. After stretching started in 4v1 box which was quite good. Encouraged to play and move so that we avoided holding the same place in the square. This made the practice a bit better and more realistic as it involved turning and calling for the ball as we moved across the square.
2	Week 2 – Wednesday. Moved to 3 v 1 in the passing practices in the 10 m box. This is necessary as having three players to hit to is too many. If your team-mates move to the full width of the box then the one defender is really stretched. What I found with this practice was that I had to be more accurate with the pass as it would travel closer to the defender. This was good as it was exactly what I needed to be practising.
3	Week 4 – Monday. We have moved to 3 v 1 playing a single touch to control and then passing when it was on. I often used something just like using a slap shot, so that there was little time spent on the preparation of the pass, time which the defenders could use to their advantage and close you down.

Explain how and why some parts of the programme were adapted as the programme progressed, or why you left the programme unchanged.

As I mentioned earlier, after the warm up I move to complete a programme of opposed practices in boxes that were designed to be realistic to the demands of a larger game of hockey. This part of the session lasted around 20 minutes with only around 3 minutes being spent on any one box practice. The remainder of the 20 minutes was spent on other skill practices such as shooting, corner drills and tackling. We trained twice a week – Monday and Wednesday.

Some relevant details about the practices are noted.

Step 1 involved us playing 4 v 1 in a box. We swapped in if our pass was poor. Play continued for a few minutes. I had to work on drawing the defender and, when the time was right, passing the ball accurately and at the right speed. This was my big concern.

In the next practice the method moved to 3 v 1. This meant that the level of opposition had increased as there were now only two other attackers to pass to. This was Step 2. Again, this practice lasted for a few minutes. This time, the task was more demanding, because the timing of passes was more important. Because the defender knew that there were only two others to pass to, it was easier for him or her to cover the passes. This occasionally resulted in me giving the ball a real belt. However, this practice was about keeping my control and passing the ball in time, without hitting it too hard and passing it to suit a shorter like setting.

Step 3 was also 3 v 1 but we were only able to take a single touch before passing. Again, this made the practice more difficult as I had even less time to pass. I had to prepare more quickly as the defender knew I had to play the ball. As the weeks went on, I moved between these steps as part of my circuits. I spent weeks 1 and 2 on Step 1, moving to Step 3 in weeks 4 and 5. Moving to the next level of opposition was not automatic. It was dependent upon the skill level which was evident in our practice.

Some useful further details on how practices functioned, particularly with regard to when and why the student moved on to the next practice stage, is useful in explaining how the level of opposition was increased.

This same idea was applied in the small-sided conditioned games that we played. Our teacher informed us that we would move on to make practice ever more game-like as it became evident that we could adapt to the new demands we were faced with. At the outset, the attacking team had an advantage in practice in that they had two additional players. This was reduced to one and then removed altogether in our small-sided games.

Slightly greater detail on why the small game part of the programme was adapted was required.

Explain how you monitored the effect of your training programme.

> One of the main ways in which the opposition practices were monitored was to study closely the effort levels of the defenders. If their effort level lowered this could be because they were either too tired or because they were giving up because they did not realistically consider that they could actually get possession of the ball. When this happens it is often time to balance the practice up by making it harder for the attackers and this is what we did by increasing the difficulty for them.
>
> The same was true, but to a lesser extent, in the conditioned games where for some reason the defenders appear to try hard at all times. Again, I think the fact that if you gained possession of the ball that you instantly became an attacker was a significant reason.

Some relevant points about how to monitor performance are explained.

Outcome 4: Evaluate the Analysis and Development Process

PC (a)   The effectiveness of the analysis and development process is discussed

PC (b)   The effects on performance are discussed

PC (c)   Future development needs are discussed

To complete the final stage of your assignment you need to reflect on the effectiveness of the programme and discuss any future development needs.

Discuss the effect that the analysis and development process had on the selected aspect of performance.

> These practices definitely helped me. I began to notice that I had become better at playing a slap shot type pass. This involved me hitting the ball with one hand at the top and one halfway down the stick, a bit like an ice hockey player would. Passing like this gave me more time and control and also meant that I did not hit the ball too hard. When I had both hands at the top of the stick I used to hit the ball too hard. This slap technique worked better as I got used to it in practice, which proves that practice is a good idea. It is also a good hitting technique as it is quite economic in that I did not swing the hockey stick too much. It also gave me a bit more time to look at the positioning of the defenders and make decisions based on where they were positioned.

A relevant explanation about the effects of improved passing technique is discussed.

Discuss the effect that the analysis and development process had on your overall performance.

> The new hitting technique has had a beneficial effect on my performance. This is evident in the accuracy and weighting of my passing in attack. In the weeks ahead I intend to complete further assessments to confirm whether this is the case when the facts are examined. However, from my reflections about my performance in games it does appear better. One benefit from the box practices was that it also helped me to improve my stickwork in preparing to pass. In the 3v1 box this had to be completed quickly in case the defender closed down on you. Improving this aspect of performance as the basis for beginning an effective pass has been useful.
>
> In games, one of the things I now concentrate on is trying to relax and pass the ball with the correct weight and timing after drawing the defender and committing them to trying to tackle. Achieving this enables my attackers to keep the attack going rather than running to retrieve the ball. Being more confident in my passing enables me to panic less when defenders begin closing me down.

Some relevant reporting about the effects of improved passing technique had on overall performance are discussed.

Discuss your future development needs in this area of performance.

> I consider that the best way to evaluate my performance and use this evidence to inform my future development needs would be to complete further similar games of hockey and record my progress against the criteria that were used for my first assessments. This would ensure that the baseline information I used at the beginning is used for later comparisons. This would give accuracy to my end-of-programme findings and provide further information about whether it was the same passing part of my game which required attention or whether it was now another aspect of performance which now required attention and training.

Brief relevant evaluation comments are provided.

When explaining the effects on performance, remind yourself of what the 'Performance Outcome' in Higher Still Physical Education mentions. It looks at 'demonstrate effective performance in challenging contexts'. It mentions, in particular, the importance of 'a broad performance repertoire', 'appropriate decisions' and 'control and fluency'. Try to link your answer to these criteria when answering Outcome 4 on 'Review the analysis and development process'.

Unit Summary: This is a mostly coherent Unit answer which is at the Unit pass standard. There is some evidence of work above the minimum standard. The thread of the answer is quite well retained as is the link between training and performance.

COURSE ASSESSMENT: STRUCTURES, STRATEGIES AND COMPOSITION (INTERMEDIATE 2 LEVEL)

(a) Choose **one** activity. Describe in detail a structure, strategy or composition you have used. **4**

(b) Describe how you **collected information** about the structure, strategy or composition you have described in part (a). **4**

(c) Explain the major **strengths** in the structure, strategy or composition you have described in part (a). **4**

(d) Explain the major weaknesses in the structure, strategy or composition you have described in part (a). **4**

(e) Describe how you evaluated the structure, strategy or composition you have described in part (a). **4**

(20)

(a) Choose **one** activity. Describe in detail a structure, strategy or composition you have used. **4**

The activity I have chosen is Badminton. As I have a good range of shots and am quite a skilful performer, able to use different technique to win points, I decided that the best strategy for me to use was to play a 'percentage game'.

The idea behind a percentage game is to play relatively safe shots and to focus on playing the shuttlecock to the corners of the opponent's court. By using such shots I can keep my opponent moving away from the centre of his or her court and so his or her chances of playing attacking shots will be reduced. This allows me to play what are called 'building shots'. These shots are used, as the name suggests, to build up attacks. For example, if I play a deep overhead clear to the back of my opponent's court, he or she might be able to play only a quite weak return to the middle of my court from where I would play a smash. The idea here is to only play a smash when it is relatively safe to do so (high percentage), as opposed to taking on more risky shots and making errors when doing so.

Teacher Example Comment
The link between technique and strategy is well made. However, some further description about the strategy (width, depth, mobility) would have been useful.

3 out of 4 marks awarded: The answer is clear and occasionally detailed.

(b)   Describe how you collected information about the structure, strategy or composition you have described in part (a).   **4**

Collecting information for this strategy was the tricky part. What I eventually decided to do, after discussing it with my teacher, was to draw out a court diagram, just like the one shown below.

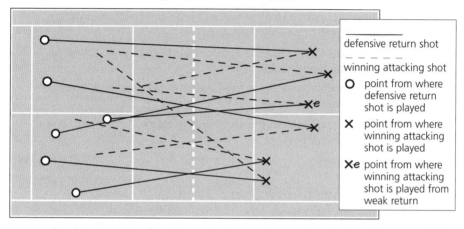

The observer marked on the court diagram from where I played the shots that lead to winning smashes. This was quite difficult for the observer to do and meant that we had to take time between points to record the details. However, this was worth doing as the examples on the diagram above show. From this data, I was able to find whether or not my building shots which lead up to smashes were helpful in winning points. This data was useful because it gave me specific information on whether or not the depth and width I was after in playing building shots to the corners was working or not.

The only difficulty with this type of data collection was what to do if my opponent played a very weak shot which allowed me to smash easily. I decided to have all my shots noted down but I made sure that my observer wrote an 'e' beside the X when a point was won from an unforced error or poor return by my opponent. This was because I really wanted to find out which points were won through my playing to my chosen strategy.

I collected data from games in which my opponents were of similar standards to me because this made my data more accurate and reliable.

The specific issues about collecting relevant data are carefully described. What separates a winning point based on strategy rather than other factors has been well thought through at the beginning.

4 marks out of 4 awarded: The student's answer is clear, full and detailed. His or her method of collecting information has been well thought through.

(c) Explain the major strengths in the structure, strategy or composition you have described in part (a).   **4**

> My main strengths in this percentage game strategy were that I was able to read different situations quite quickly and play a range of shots which helped put my strategy into practice. For example, I was able to think through whether to play a low net return or a high clear to the back of the court in good time. These decisions were based on where my opponent was positioned. This improved my confidence in using the strategy. As a result, I did not force the play too much. One possible problem with this strategy is that if you try to play to the corners too much, then you can hit the shuttle out of the court and lose games through making unforced or unnecessary errors.
>
> My main strength was that I was able to play to safe areas of the court without unforced errors such as hitting the shuttle out of the court. This was achieved mostly by hitting down the line rather than across the court. When I hit across the court, my opponent often had the chance to step across and play the shuttle away from me and win the point outright.

The game examples of the student's strengths in action are well explained. Some further links to how these strengths linked to the strategy were required.

2 marks out of 4 awarded: The answer uses a wide range of relevant concepts to make sound judgements.

(d) Explain the major weaknesses in the structure, strategy or composition you have described in part (a).   **4**

> My major weaknesses were that I was weak at hitting the shuttle across the width of the back line when hitting it to the back of the court and that I did not use deception enough.
>
> The first weakness meant that when I was playing clears to the back of the court, I would hit them down the middle of the court too often. I was therefore not using the width of the court as well I might have done, even though I was using the depth of the court well. This meant that my opponent could return my shots with overhead forehand shots. This is quite a strong shot whereas an overhead backhand shot is weaker. What I needed to do more was to play the shuttle over to the back of the court on my

opponent's backhand side so that I could force him or her into playing a weaker overhead backhand return. The results of playing better building shots were that it was easier for me to play winning shots from them.

My other weakness was that I did not manage to use deception enough. Often it is pretty clear to my opponent what type of shot I am going to play and where I am about to play it to. This means that my play is rather predictable and that at times my opponent can play attacking shots from my building shots.

The game examples of the student's weaknesses in action are well explained. On this occasion there are some better links to how these strengths weaknesses related to the strategy.

3 marks out of 4 awarded: The student has used a range of relevant concepts to make sound judgements.

(e) Describe how you evaluated the structure, strategy or composition you
have described in part (a).   **4**

For my evaluation, it was important to me to compare how well I had done at the end of the season in comparison with how well I had done at the beginning. This would allow me see whether or not I had improved. For this reason, I decided to evaluate my performance again by completing a further observation schedule that used the same court details as used on the first occasion. I ensured that my re-observation was recorded during a game against a player of similar ability, and in the same type of singles competitive game, as when my initial observation was recorded. This ensured my results were accurate and useful to my evaluation. It allowed me to compare my later information, following my training programme, against my baseline information from before my training programme. I wanted to see whether more of my winning smashes resulted from playing building shots that were deeper or wider than before, while still being high percentage shots because I had managed to avoid hitting them out of the court.

The evaluation of performance is well explained. Again, a clearer link to the strategy being followed would have helped the quality of the evaluation explanation.

3 marks out of 4 awarded: The student's answer contains a clear and full description of the evaluation process.

Total: 15 marks out of 20 awarded

Conclusion

I hope through studying *Intermediate 2 and Higher Level Physical Education Grade Booster* that you have been able to connect your learning in school with the the key stages involved in analysing and developing your performance.

If you have taken time to complete this journey, and can link the analysis process with the practical activities you participate in as part of your Higher Still course, you are in a great position to achieve the best grade possible.

Passing Intermediate 2 and Higher level Physical Education can open up tremendous opportunites in life for you, both in terms of studying in further and higher education and of pursuing a career in sport related industries. It also shows how interested you are in active living, in participating in a range of sports and in studying at Intermediate 2 and Higher level.

Achieving the best grade possible is rarely down to luck and good fortune. Making the most of your potential is about making chances and then taking them. I hope your detailed studying and engagement with *Intermediate 2 and Higher Level Physical Education Grade Booster* provides you with the chance to realise your potential to the full.

Key Words Checklist

It is important that you have a good working vocabulary of words and their meanings. Check that you are familiar with the meanings of the words below, which relate to the different Key Concepts.

Key Concepts	Key words
Performance Appreciation	
Overall nature and demands of quality performance	'experiential' 'precision' 'control' 'accuracy'
Technical, physical, personal and special qualities of performance	'emotional control' 'codes of conduct' 'imagination' 'flair' 'creativity'
Mental factors influencing performance	'motivation' 'managing stress' 'self-confidence' 'comfort zone' 'visualisation'
The use of appropriate models of performance	'personal style' 'mental imagery'
Planning and managing personal performance improvement	'on-going monitoring of performance' 'setting performance goals'
Preparation of the Body	
Fitness assessment in relation to personal performance and the demands of activities	'standardised procedures' 'regular monitoring of performance' 'test norms'
Application of different types of fitness in the development of activity specific performance	'performance review' 'conditioning training'
Physical, skill-related and mental aspects of fitness	'speed endurance' 'strength endurance' 'dynamic strength' 'local muscular endurance' 'flexibility' 'reaction time' 'agility' 'balance' 'movement anticipation' 'co-ordination' 'level of arousal' 'rehearsal' 'managing your emotions'
Principles and methods of training	'specificity' 'progressive overload' 'intensity' 'duration' 'frequency' 'combined skill and fitness training programmes' 'adaptation' 'reversibility'

Key Concepts	Key words
Planning, implementing and monitoring training	'identifiable goals' 'short- and long-term goals' 'periodisation' 'peaking for performance' 'tapering down' 'phases of training' 'training cycles' 'monitoring performance'
Skills and Techniques	
The concepts of skill and skilled performance	'fluent controlled movements' 'selecting correct options' 'skills which reflect experience and ability' 'information processing' 'learning loop' 'decision-making' 'open and closed skills' 'simple and complex skills' ' discrete / serial and continuous skills' 'variations in technique'
Skill / technique improvement through mechanical analysis or movement analysis or consideration of quality	'force' 'body levers' 'planes of movement' 'preparation, action and recovery' 'managing effort factors in performance' 'personal and technical qualities'
The development of skill and the refinement of technique	'preparation, practice and automatic stages of learning' 'solo / shadow / partner / group practice' 'opposed / unopposed practice' 'repetition / drills practice' 'massed / distributed practice' 'conditioned games / small-sided games' 'whole / part / whole practice' ' work to rest ratios' 'progression' 'internal motivation' 'goal setting' 'external motivation' 'concentration' 'forms of feedback' 'knowledge of results' 'effect of boredom and fatigue'
Structures, Strategies and Composition	
The structures, strategies and / or compositional elements that are fundamental to activities	'tempo' 'deception' 'design form and style with a composition'
Identification of strengths and weaknesses in performance in terms of: roles and relationships, formations, tactical or design elements and choreography	'support' 'continuity' 'pressure' 'improvisation' 'cohesion' 'width' 'depth' 'mobility' 'systems of play' 'positive team/group ethos' 'interpreting stimulus' 'timing' 'improvisation'
Information processing, problem-solving and decision-making when working to develop and improve performance	'adapting and refining' 'individual and group decision-making' 'dynamics and relationships' 'effective decision-making under pressure'

Final Examination Preparation

As you prepare for your final examination it is useful to note down the key points you wish to include in your answers. The following preparation sheets are designed to help you plan your answer. The task is to note down the three most important points you want to include in your answer for each of the four learning outcomes. Complete three preparation sheets, one for each of the areas of analysis and development of performance answers you will write about in your examination.

Activity: _____

Area of Analysis and Development of Performance: _____

Evaluate

Investigate

Develop

Analyse

Activity: _____

Area of Analysis and Development of Performance: _____

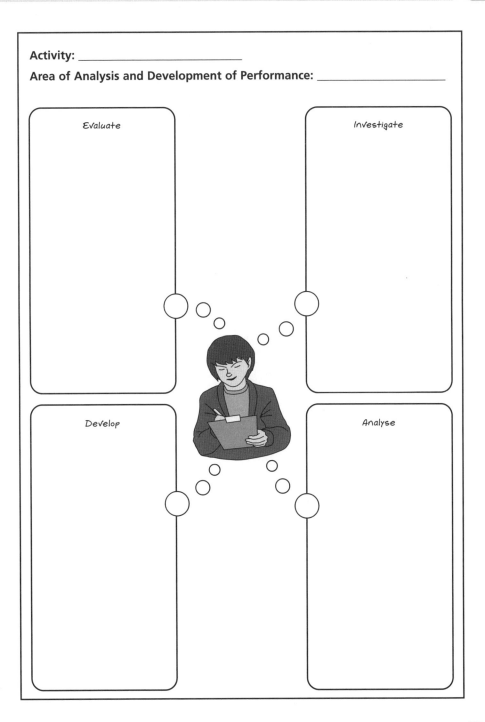

Evaluate

Investigate

Develop

Analyse

Activity: _____

Area of Analysis and Development of Performance: _____

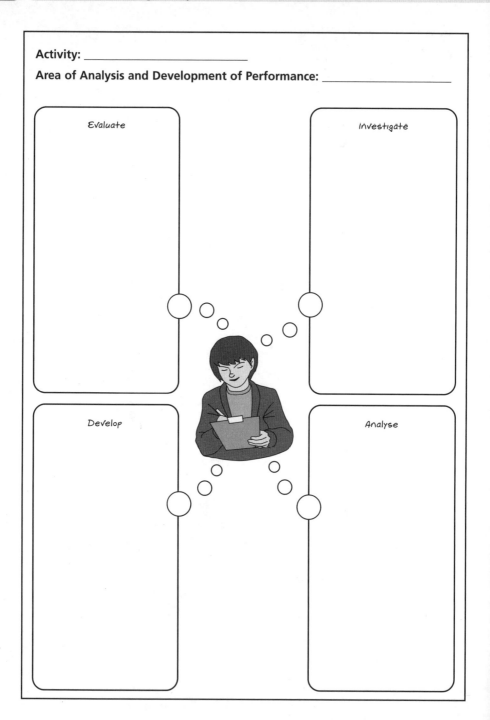

Evaluate

Investigate

Develop

Analyse